QUILTED FOR CHRISTMAS

BOOK IV

COMPILED BY JANET WHITE

Contributors

Roxanne Carter ❖ Carol Doak

Linda Gabrielse ❖ Dixie Haywood

Gretchen Kluth Hudock

Angela Krotowski

Deborah J. Moffett-Hall

Barbara Nienow

Lezette Thomason

Mary Ellen Von Holt

Eileen Westfall ❖ Tonee White

Retta Warehime

That Patchwork Place

CREDITS

Editor-in-Chief ....Kerry I. Smith
Technical Editor .... Janet White
Managing Editor ....Judy Petry
Copy Editor ....Tina Cook
Proofreader ....Leslie Phillips
Design Director ....Cheryl Stevenson
Cover Designer ....Barbara Schmitt
Text Designer ....Kay Green
Production Assistant ....Claudia L'Heureux
Illustrator ....Laurel Strand
Photographer ....Brent Kane

Quilted for Christmas, Book IV
©1997 by That Patchwork Place, Inc.
PO Box 1930, Woodinville, WA 98072-1930 USA

Printed in Hong Kong
02 01 00 99 98 97   6 5 4 3 2 1

The information in this book is presented in good faith, but no warranty is given nor results guaranteed. Since That Patchwork Place, Inc., has no control over choice of materials or procedures, the company assumes no responsibility for the use of this information.

Background paper made by Cheryl Stevenson, Dancing Cat Paperworks.

Library of Congress Cataloging-in-Publication Data
Quilted for Christmas, Book IV /
    p.   cm.
    ISBN 1-56477-054-0 :
    1. Patchwork quilts. 2. Quilting—Patterns. 3. Appliqué.
    4. Christmas decorations.
TT835.Q5357 1994
746.9'7—dc20   93-44135
                                                      CIP
This volume: ISBN 1-56477-186-5

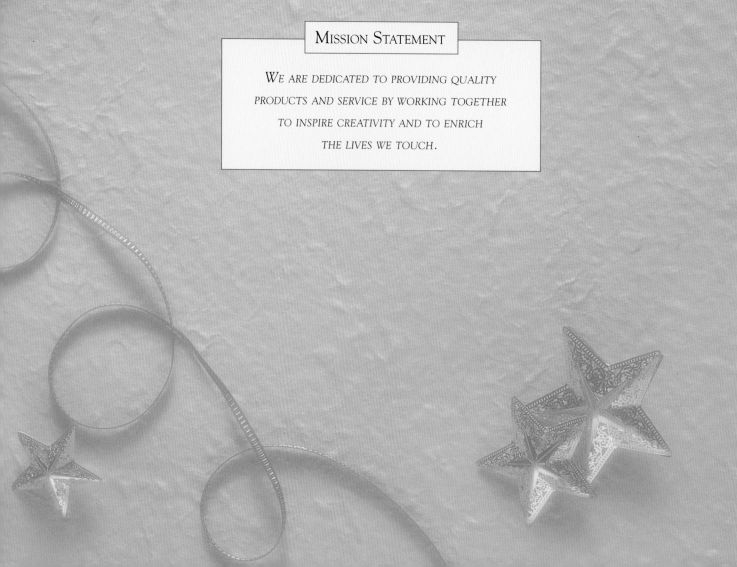

MISSION STATEMENT

WE ARE DEDICATED TO PROVIDING QUALITY
PRODUCTS AND SERVICE BY WORKING TOGETHER
TO INSPIRE CREATIVITY AND TO ENRICH
THE LIVES WE TOUCH.

Table of Contents

Introduction

Christmas is a time to share your love with friends and family, and what better way than with a gift you've made. In *Quilted for Christmas, Book IV*, we've brought together a collection of Christmas treats for the eye and the heart by designers from Canada and all over the United States. Add holiday cheer to your home or the home of someone you love with a quilt, tree skirt, banner, or pillow.

These charming quilted projects will appeal to quilters with a wide range of skill levels. Techniques include hand appliqué, rotary cutting and speed piecing, embroidery, and foundation piecing. Begin right now, and you'll have plenty of time to make holiday gifts for the special ones in your life, and something for yourself too.

Janet White

Crowning Glory

By Roxanne Carter

Crowning Glory by Roxanne Carter, 1996, Mukilteo, Washington, 48" x 48".

ROXANNE HAS BEEN SEWING SINCE SHE WAS FIVE YEARS OLD, BUT SHE REALLY GOT INTERESTED IN QUILTING IN 1980, WHEN SHE TOOK HER FIRST SAMPLER CLASS. SHE STARTED TO TEACH QUILTING WHEN SHE MOVED TO WASHINGTON STATE SEVEN YEARS AGO. ROXANNE TEACHES AN AVERAGE OF THREE CLASSES A WEEK, AND SHE SHARES HER LOVE OF QUILTING WITH HER STUDENTS AND FAMILY MEMBERS. SHE IS ALWAYS LOOKING FOR A FASTER, EASIER WAY TO DO A PROJECT AND ENJOYS TEACHING THESE NEW TECHNIQUES TO HER STUDENTS.

IT WAS DURING A TEACHING ADVENTURE THAT ROXANNE CAME UP WITH THE DESIGN FOR CROWNING GLORY. ONCE A MONTH SHE TEACHES A CLASS CALLED GIRLS NITE OUT, AND IN EACH CLASS THE STUDENTS MAKE A DIFFERENT PROJECT. THEY WANTED TO LEARN HOW TO MAKE THE DRUNKARD'S PATH SHAPE, SO ROXANNE DESIGNED A DRUNKARD'S PATH BORDER FOR HER FAVORITE BLOCK, THE FEATHERED STAR. THE BACKGROUND BLOCKS AND CORNER TRIANGLES GIVE QUILTERS AMPLE OPPORTUNITY TO SHOW OFF THEIR STITCHING.

Quilt Size: 48" x 48"

Materials: 42"-wide fabric

1 yd. Christmas print

1 yd. red for star feathers,
border, and binding

¾ yd. white for star background

¾ yd. green for star and curved border

½ yd. dark pink for curved inner border

⅝ yd. light pink for corner triangles

6

Making the Feathered Star Medallion
Cutting

Fabric	Piece	Cut
Christmas print	A	1 square, 7" x 7"
	C	4 squares, each 5½" x 5½"; cut each square once diagonally to make 8 triangles
Red	E	1 strip, 1⅝" x 42"
	I	8 squares, each 1⅝" x 1⅝"
	Bias Squares	1 strip, 7" x 22"
White	F	8 squares, each 2" x 2"; cut each square once diagonally to make 16 triangles
	G	4 squares, each 6¾" x 6¾"
	H	1 square, 10" x 10"; cut twice diagonally to make 4 triangles
	Bias Squares	1 strip, 7" x 22"
Green	B	4 squares, each 2⅜" x 2⅜"
	D	1 square, 4" x 4"; cut twice diagonally to make 4 triangles

Bias Squares

1. Pair the red and white 7" x 22" strips, right sides together. Draw a true bias line on the top fabric, using a ruler with a 45° angle line. Cut 7 bias strips parallel to the drawn line, each 1⅝" wide.

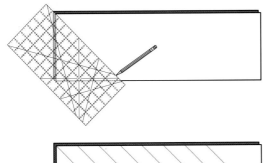

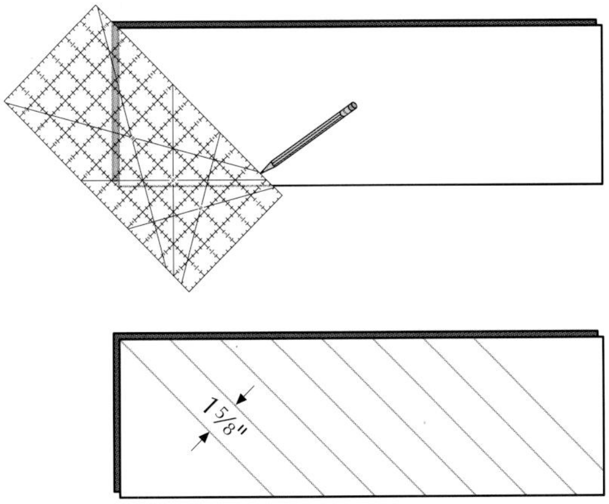

2. Using a ¼"-wide seam allowance, sew each pair of strips together along both long sides.
3. Using a Bias Square® ruler, cut one end of each strip at a 45° angle.

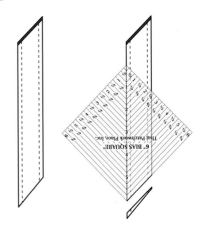

4. To cut a 1⅝" bias square, place the 45°-angle line of the Bias Square on the seam of a strip, aligning the 1⅝" mark with the cut end of the strip. Turn the strip over and cut another bias square in the same way. Cut 48 bias squares. Press each square open and trim off the "ears."

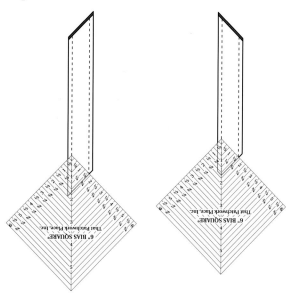

5. Trim the selvage end of the 1⅝" x 42" red strip at a 45° angle. Align a ruler's 45°-angle line with the long edge of the strip and the 1⅝" line with the cut edge of the strip. Cut 8 diamonds, each 1⅝" wide, to make piece E.

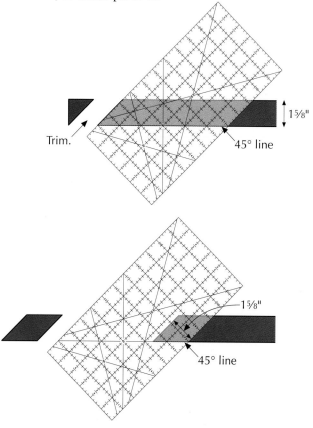

Corner Units

1. Mark the intersections of the ¼"-wide seam allowances on all triangles and diamond pieces.
2. Arrange 6 bias squares, 1 red square (I), 2 white triangles (F), 2 red diamonds (E), and 1 white square (G) as shown. Be sure to position the bias squares correctly. Sew the small squares, triangles, and diamonds into 2 strips. Sew the strips to the large square, pressing the seams toward the square. Make 4 corner units.

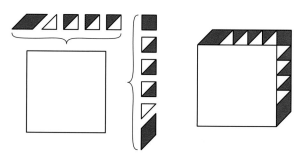

Side Units

1. Arrange 6 bias squares, 1 red triangle (I), and 2 white triangles (F), on the 2 short sides of a large white triangle (H). Be sure to position the bias squares correctly. Sew the squares and small triangles into 2 strips. Sew the strips to the large triangle, leaving the seam partially unsewn as indicated. Make 4 units.

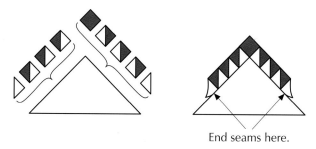

End seams here.

2. Align the long edge of a triangle C with a ruler, placing the left corner at the ruler's 5½" mark. Cut along the edge of the ruler to trim. Repeat with all 8 of the C triangles. This piece is symmetrical, so there is no need to cut a reversed shape.

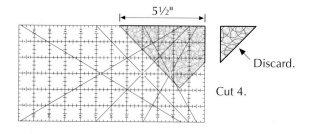

3. Sew a piece C to the left side of each unit made in step 1.
4. Sew each triangle D to a piece C. Sew this unit to the right side of a unit made in step 3 to complete the side unit. Make 4.

Center Unit

Mark a diagonal line on the wrong side of each small white square (B), from corner to corner. Place a marked square on a corner of the large center square (A), right sides together. Stitch on the diagonal line and trim the seam allowance to ¹/4". Press the triangle toward the corner. Repeat with the remaining marked squares on the other 3 corners of the large square.

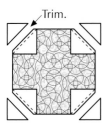
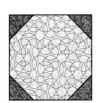

Center Unit
Make 1.

Block Assembly

1. Arrange the units as shown.

2. Sew the units together in horizontal rows. To join the corner and side units, first sew the side of the corner unit to the side unit, matching the ¹/4" marks. Stop stitching at the ¹/4" mark on the diamond. Finish the remainder of the half seam along the large triangle. Join the rows to complete the Feathered Star medallion.

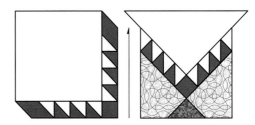

Stitch from corner to seam intersection.

Complete the seam.

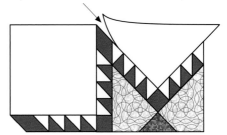

Adding Borders
Cutting

Fabric	Piece	Cut
Christmas print	Outer border	6 strips, each 4½" x 42"
Red	Border flap	4 strips, each 1¼" x 42"
	Binding	5 strips, each 2½" x 42"
White	Drunkard's Path border	6 squares, each 4¾" x 4¾"; cut each square twice diagonally to make 24 triangles
		4 Template A*
Green	Outer border	4 strips, each 2" x 42"
	Drunkard's Path border	7 squares, each 6" x 6"
		8 Template A*
Dark pink	Drunkard's Path border	7 squares, each 4¾" x 4¾"; cut each square twice diagonally to make 28 triangles
		8 squares, each 6" x 6"
		3 Template A*
Light pink	Large triangles	2 squares, each 18¼" x 18¼"; cut each square once diagonally to make 4 triangles

Use the template on page 11.

Drunkard's Path Border

1. Using the template on page 11, trace 15 circles onto the dull side of freezer paper and cut them out. Press the shiny side of each circle to the wrong side of the appropriate fabric: 4 each on white and dark pink, and 8 on green. Cut around each circle, adding a ¼"-wide seam allowance. Fold the seam allowance to the paper side of each circle, gluing in place with a gluestick, or, if you prefer, basting around the edge. Fold each circle in half twice, creasing the paper sharply to mark the center.

2. Fold each 6" square in half twice, creasing to mark the center. Place a circle on a square, matching the centers. Pin the circle in several places to hold it firm. Appliqué the circles to the squares by hand or by machine.

Make 4 green squares with white circles. Make 3 green squares with dark pink circles. Make 8 dark pink squares with green circles.

3. Cut each square in half twice to make 4 Drunkard's Path units, each 3" x 3", for a total of 60 units.

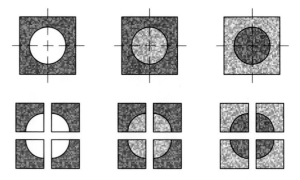

4. Sew the white and dark pink triangles and the Drunkard's Path units together as shown to make 4 inner borders.

5. Pin the inner borders to the sides of the Feathered Star medallion so that the white triangles are next to the star. Match the seam intersections at the corners of the medallion to the white triangle points at the ends of each border. Sew from seam intersection to seam intersection, backstitching at each end.

6. Sew the ends of the border strips together, matching the circles.

7. Sew a light pink triangle to each side of the Feathered Star medallion.

8. For the border flap, fold each 1¼"-wide red strip in half lengthwise, wrong sides together, and press.

9. Baste a folded strip to the right side of one long side of each 2"-wide green strip, using a seam allowance a little less than ¼"-wide.

10. Cut 2 of the 4½"-wide Christmas print strips in half and piece 1 short strip to each remaining long strip.

11. Sew a pieced print strip to each green border strip, right sides together, sandwiching the flap between them. Sew a border unit to each side of the quilt top, starting and stopping your stitching

¼" from each end. Miter the corners, referring to "Mitered-Corner Borders" on pages 84–85.

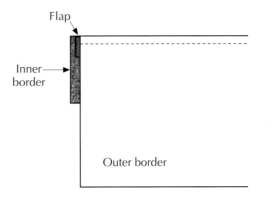

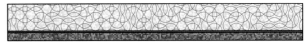

Finishing

For detailed finishing instructions, refer to pages 85–87.

1. Mark the quilt top with desired quilting patterns.
2. Layer the quilt top with batting and backing; baste.
3. Quilt on the marked lines.
4. Add a hanging sleeve if desired.
5. Using the 2½"-wide red strips, bind the edges with double-fold binding.
6. Label your quilt.

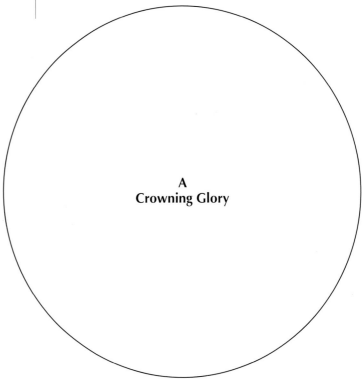

A
Crowning Glory

X's and O's

By Dixie Haywood

X's and O's by Dixie Haywood, 1993, Pensacola, Florida, 46" x 46".

DIXIE HAYWOOD

DIXIE HAYWOOD'S TALENTED MOTHER TAUGHT HER TO SEW, AND DIXIE MADE HER FIRST GARMENT AT THE AGE OF EIGHT. QUILTMAKING OPENED A NEW WORLD, WHICH DIXIE SHARES WITH OTHERS WHENEVER POSSIBLE. IN ADDITION TO TEACHING AND JUDGING, SHE HELPED FOUND THREE QUILT GUILDS IN DIFFERENT AREAS OF THE COUNTRY. SHE HAS WRITTEN FIVE BOOKS AND REGULARLY CONTRIBUTES ARTICLES AND DESIGNS TO LEADING QUILTING PUBLICATIONS. MANY OF HER QUILTS HAVE WON AWARDS, BUT THE PROCESS OF QUILTMAKING, FROM DESIGN TO FINAL STITCH, GIVES HER THE MOST PLEASURE. SHE ESPECIALLY ENJOYS USING CONTEMPORARY TECHNIQUES AND INNOVATIVE APPROACHES TO ADAPT TRADITIONAL DESIGNS.

A NATIVE OF WASHINGTON STATE, DIXIE NOW LIVES IN PENSACOLA, FLORIDA, AFTER A LIFE-TIME OF MOVES FOR HER HUSBAND'S CAREER AS A MILITARY AND CIVILIAN METEOROLOGIST. SHE HAS TWO SONS, A DAUGHTER, AND THREE GRANDSONS. THESE THIRD-GENERATION QUILT LOVERS ALREADY OWN NINE QUILTS AMONG THEM.

"X'S AND O'S" IS PART OF A SE-RIES THAT EXPLORES DIFFERENT ASPECTS OF YELLOW AND VARIATIONS OF THE WAGON WHEEL BLOCK. IN THIS QUILT, THE PATTERN WAS ABSTRACTED TO ITS BASIC ELEMENTS. THE LINES OF THE PAT-TERN SUGGEST WRAPPED PACKAGES. THE TITLE REFERS BOTH TO THE CROSSED LINES OF THE PATTERN AND TO THE GREET-INGS WE LOOK FORWARD TO DURING THE HOLIDAY SEASON.

Quilt Size: 46" x 46"

Materials: 42"-wide fabric

3/4 yd. green print for narrow strips (D and D reversed) and inner border

1/2 yd. red plaid for large quarter-circles (A) and outer border

5/8 yd. red print for arc (B), small quarter-circle (E), and binding

1/2 yd. gold print for block sides (C)

1/3 yd. red stripe for wide strip (F) and corners (H) (Note: Same yardage for cross-grain stripes)

2/3 yd. gold stripe for wide strip (G) and corners (H) (Note: 1/2 yd. for cross-grain stripes)

2 5/8 yds. for backing

54" x 54" piece of batting

Cutting for Borders

*Cut the following borders and binding
before cutting the block pieces:*

From the green print, cut:
  8 strips, each 4" x 23½"
From the red plaid, cut on the same plaid lines:
  4 strips, each 2" x 40"
  4 strips, each 2" x 8"
From the red print, cut:
  5 strips, each 2" x 40", for binding

Cutting for Blocks

Use the templates on the pullout.

Fabric	Piece	No. to Cut	Dimensions
Green print	D, D reversed	16 each	
Red plaid	A	16	
Red print	B, E	16 each	
Gold print	C	16	
Red stripe	F	8 each	3" x 9⅝"
	H*	8	4¼" x 4¼"; cut each square once diagonally to make 16 triangles
Gold stripe	G	4	3" x 21⅜"
	H*	16	4¼" x 4¼"; cut each square once diagonally to make 16 triangles

*Cut piece H so the stripe will form an interesting pattern when four triangles meet. This may cause the triangles to be off-grain, so handle them with care to avoid stretching.

Making the Blocks

1. Sew each arc (B) to a quarter-circle (A). Press the seam allowance toward (A).

2. Sew a side piece (C) to each A-B unit. Press the seam allowance toward the A-B unit.

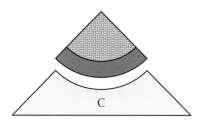

3. Sew the D and D reversed strips to the sides of the unit, pressing the seam allowances toward the strips.

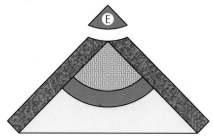

4. Add the small quarter-circle (E) as shown. (It is easier to appliqué this small piece, although it can be pieced.)

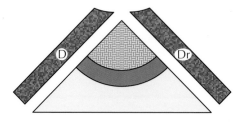

5. Sew a completed unit to each long side of the F strips; then sew 1 of these sections to each long side of the G strips. Press the seam allowances toward the strips. Add the red stripe H triangles to the corners to complete the blocks, matching the triangles to the adjacent strips. Press the seam allowances toward the triangles.

Making the Inner Border

1. Trim the right end of 4 green border strips at a 45° angle. Trim the left end of the remaining strips. Sew a gold stripe H triangle to the angled end of each strip.

2. Sew the strips together to form 4 border strips, triangles matching at the centers.

Assembling the Quilt Top

1. Sew the 4 blocks together.

2. Sew a 2" x 8" red plaid strip to each 2" x 40" red plaid strip to make 4 outer border strips.

3. Sew an outer border strip to each pieced, inner border strip, matching the centers.

4. Referring to "Mitered-Corner Borders" on pages 84–85, add the borders to the quilt, matching the border triangles to those on the quilt top.

Finishing

For detailed finishing instructions, refer to pages 85–87.

1. Mark the quilt top with desired quilting patterns.
2. Layer the quilt top with batting and backing; baste.
3. Add a hanging sleeve if desired.
4. Bind and label your quilt.

Holiday Wreath

By Linda Gabrielse

Holiday Wreath by Linda Gabrielse, 1996, Kentwood, Michigan, 34" x 34".

LINDA GABRIELSE

LINDA HAS BEEN QUILTING FOR ABOUT TWELVE YEARS AND TEACHING FOR EIGHT. SHE LIKES ALL ASPECTS OF QUILTMAKING, ESPECIALLY HAND APPLIQUÉ, HAND PIECING, AND DIMENSIONAL AND EMBROIDERED EMBELLISHMENTS. SHE ESPECIALLY ENJOYS SHARING HER QUILTMAKING TECHNIQUES WITH STUDENTS. IN FACT, LINDA THINKS OF THE INSPIRATION SHE RECEIVES FROM HER STUDENTS AND TEACHERS AS GIFTS.

LINDA CREDITS HER MOTHER AND GRANDMOTHERS FOR HER LOVE OF NEEDLE ARTS. AS A YOUNG GIRL, LINDA LOVED WATCHING HER GRANDMOTHERS AS THEY TATTED, KNITTED, AND CROCHETED, AND SHE LEARNED TO DO ALL THREE. SHE GAINED HER LOVE OF FLOWERS, COLOR, AND EMBROIDERY FROM HER MOTHER. HER DEVOTION TO QUILTING BEGAN IN 1984 WHEN SHE SAW A CHRISTMAS WALL HANGING SHE WANTED. SHE SIGNED UP FOR THE CLASS AND HAS BEEN QUILTING EVER SINCE.

LINDA BEGAN DESIGNING HER OWN PATTERNS IN 1988. SHE IS ACTIVE IN THE WEST MICHIGAN QUILTER'S GUILD, AND WAS RECENTLY ASKED TO SERVE ON THE BOARD OF THE NATIONAL QUILTING ASSOCIATION, INC., AS MEMBERSHIP CHAIR. SHE TEACHES QUILTING NEAR HOME AND TAUGHT FOR THE AMERICAN QUILTER'S SOCIETY IN PADUCAH, KENTUCKY, IN 1995, AND FOR THE NATIONAL QUILTING ASSOCIATION, INC., SHOW IN 1996.

LINDA DESIGNED "HOLIDAY WREATH" IN THE SPRING OF 1996. SHE HAS ALWAYS LOVED BOTH CHRISTMAS AND HEARTS. THIS DESIGN PROJECT PROVIDED A WAY TO USE BOTH.

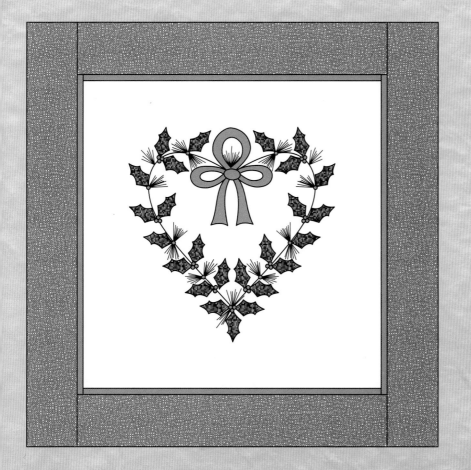

Quilt Size: 34" x 34"

Materials: 42"-wide fabric

7/8 yd. white solid for background

1/3 yd. green print for holly leaves

1/4 yd. red #1 for holly berries and bow

1/4 yd. red #2 for inner border

5/8 yd. print #1 for outer border

1/2 yd. print #2 for binding

1 1/4 yds. fabric for backing

38" x 38" piece of low-loft batting

10" x 10" piece of cotton batting for stuffed berries

Embroidery floss in black and green

Cutting

Use the templates on page 88. Use your favorite method to cut and prepare the appliqués.

From the white solid, cut:
  1 piece, 28" x 28", for the center panel

From the green print, cut:
  25 holly leaves

From red #1, cut:
  1 each of Bow templates 1 and 1 reversed, 2 and 2 reversed, 3, and 4

From red #2, cut:
  2 strips, each 1" x 25$\frac{1}{2}$"
  2 strips, each 1" x 26$\frac{1}{2}$"

From the Christmas print, cut:
  2 strips, each 4$\frac{1}{2}$" x 26$\frac{1}{2}$"
  2 strips, each 4$\frac{1}{2}$" x 34$\frac{1}{2}$"

Making the Wreath

1. Using the pattern on the pullout, trace half the heart onto a 15" x 15" piece of tracing paper. Turn over the tracing paper (you may need to mark the line on the other side), and trace the other side of the heart onto the tracing paper. Trace the complete heart onto freezer paper.

2. Center the freezer-paper heart on the 28" white square, shiny side down. Press the heart onto the fabric.

3. Mark around the freezer-paper template with a fine-line pencil; Linda prefers a 0.5mm mechanical pencil. Remove the freezer paper. Trace the necessary placement lines for the holly leaves, pine needles, and bow. Linda used a black 0.1 Pigma® pen to give the needles depth without adding bulk.

4. Appliqué the bow pieces to the background in numerical order.

5. Beginning at the bottom point of the heart, embroider the heart outline, using a chain stitch and 1 strand of each floss color.

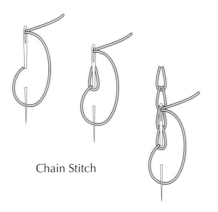

Chain Stitch

6. Appliqué the holly leaves around the heart shape.

7. Using 1 strand of green embroidery floss, stem-stitch the pine needles.

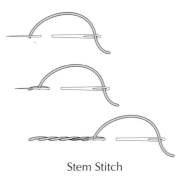

Stem Stitch

Making Stuffed Berries

1. Using the berry template on the pullout or a dime, mark 35 berries on the red fabric. Leave enough space between each berry to add scant $\frac{3}{16}$"-wide seam allowances.

2. Cut out each berry, adding a scant $\frac{3}{16}$"-wide seam allowance. Linda cuts out and makes 1 berry at a time so she doesn't lose any.

3. Using a double strand of quilting thread that matches your berries, turn under the seam allowance and sew a running stitch around the berry, making sure the thread knot is inside the berry.

4. Gently draw up the quilting thread so the berry forms a small cup.

5. Pinch off a small amount of cotton batting and roll it into a ball; cotton compresses best. Place the batting ball inside the cupped berry, it should overfill the cup slightly.

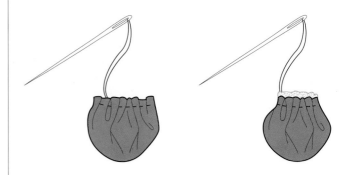

6. Draw up the quilting thread tightly around the filled berry. Roll the berry between your thumb and first two fingers as you draw up the thread to ensure that your berry will be firm and round. Knot the thread, but don't cut it. If there is still some batting showing, or if the berry has ridges, stitch back and forth across the bottom of the berry to close it and firm it up.

7. Referring to the template on the pullout for placement, stitch the berries onto the wreath.

Finishing

For detailed finishing instructions, refer to pages 85–87.

1. Trim the white center panel to 25½" x 25½".
2. Referring to "Straight-Cut Borders" on page 84, sew the 1"-wide red #2 strips and the 4½"-wide Christmas print borders to the quilt top.
3. Layer the quilt top with batting and backing; baste.
4. Quilt the wreath as desired. Linda quilted vertical lines outside the wreath, ¾" apart. She quilted the inner border in-the-ditch; the diagonal lines in the outer border are 1" apart.
5. Add a hanging sleeve if desired.
6. Bind the edges of the quilt with 1¼"-wide straight-grain strips of print #2.
7. Label your quilt.

Christmas Tulips

By Angela Krotowski

Christmas Tulips by Angela Krotowski, December 1990, Aurora, Ontario, Canada, 84" x 84".

ANGELA FIRST BEGAN QUILTING IN 1974. HER QUILTS HAVE WON NUMEROUS AWARDS AND RIBBONS, INCLUDING FIRST PRIZE AT QUILT EXPO '96, BEST OF SHOW AT PRINCE EDWARD COUNTY QUILT GUILD, AND SECOND PRIZE AT COUNTRY QUILT FEST '96. HER LOVE OF QUILTING HAS LED HER TO DESIGN HER OWN PATTERNS AND TO TEACH AND LECTURE. ONE OF HER AWARD-WINNING DESIGNS WAS INCLUDED IN THAT PATCHWORK PLACE'S CLASS-ACT QUILTS. SHE TEACHES THE MANY FACETS OF QUILTING AT DIFFERENT GUILDS, AT QUILT SHOPS, AND IN HER OWN HOME. HER TRUNK SHOW IS APTLY NAMED "MY BEGINNINGS AND NEVER ENDINGS," BECAUSE FOR EVERY QUILT ANGELA FINISHES, THERE ARE UNTOLD NUMBERS ON THE WAY.

ANGELA IS ACTIVE IN MANY ASPECTS OF QUILTING. SHE IS CURRENTLY INVOLVED IN A PROGRAM OF HER OWN CALLED "QUILT FROM THE HEART," IN WHICH QUILTERS MEET AT HER HOUSE ON A MONTHLY BASIS TO MAKE QUILTS FOR WOMEN'S SHELTERS. NOT ONLY HAS ANGELA BROUGHT QUILTING ACTIVITIES TO THE LOCAL SENIOR CENTER AND HER CHURCH GROUP, BUT SHE HAS ALSO UNDERTAKEN THE TASK OF MAKING A HISTORICAL QUILT CELEBRATING THE 200TH ANNIVERSARY OF THE LONGEST STREET IN THE WORLD, ONTARIO'S YONGE STREET, 1,178 MILES LONG. SHE ALSO COORDINATED THE WORK OF FIFTY QUILTERS WHO MADE A HISTORICAL QUILT FOR HER HOMETOWN. ANGELA IS INVOLVED WITH THE REGION OF YORK QUILTERS GUILD AND HAS BEEN HONORED WITH A LIFETIME MEMBERSHIP FOR HER MANY CONTRIBUTIONS TO THE GUILD.

ANGELA'S QUILTS ARE TRADITIONAL AND MADE FOR MANY OF THE SAME REASONS OUR ANCESTORS QUILTED. TRADITIONAL ROOTS ARE EVIDENT EVEN IN HER ORIGINAL DESIGNS. HER FAVORITE TIME FOR QUILTING IS THE WINTER, SO HER DESIGNS OFTEN HAVE A CHRISTMAS LOOK. SHE SAYS, "I TRY TO LET MY LOVE FOR THE PEACE AND SERENITY OF THE CHRISTMAS SEASON SHOW IN MY QUILTS. NO MATTER HOW FRANTIC OR STRESSFUL LIFE GETS, QUILTING PROVIDES ME WITH CALM AND EASES THE SNAGS THAT COME UP IN EVERYDAY LIVING."

Quilt Size: 84" x 84"

Materials: 42"-wide fabric

12 yds. muslin for background and backing

3 yds. red solid for sashing, swags, bows, and flowers

¾ yd. gold solid for setting squares and flower petals

½ yd. gold print for tulips

2 yds. green print for tulips, inner border, and binding

88" x 88" piece of batting

Cutting

Use the templates on pages 89–90.

From the muslin, cut:

4 squares, each 12½" x 12½", for Tulip blocks

2 squares, each 18½" x 18½"; cut each square twice diagonally to make 8 triangles

9 Template 2

4 Template 2a

4 Template 2b

84 Template 8 for inner border

8 Template 9 for inner border

2 strips from the lengthwise grain, each 15" x 56", for outer border

2 strips from the lengthwise grain, each 15" x 86", for outer border

From the red solid, cut:

16 pieces each, 4½" x 12½", for sashing

4 each Template 11 and 11 reversed for corner swags

8 Template 12

32 Template 13

16 Template 14

4 Template 2

8 Template 2a

96 Template 1

From the gold solid, cut:

9 squares, each 4½" x 4½", for sashing

2 squares, each 3¾" x 3¾"; cut each square once diagonally to make 8 triangles

1 square, 7" x 7"; cut twice diagonally to make 4 triangles

64 Template 1

From the gold print, cut:

56 Template 3 tulip centers

8 each Template 3a and 3a reversed tulip half-centers

From the green print, cut:

64 each Template 4 and 4 reversed

84 Template 8 for inner border

8 Template 9 for inner border

56 bias strips, each 1⅛" x 4", for stems

Making the Appliqué Blocks

Use the placement guide on pages 89–90.

Tulip Block

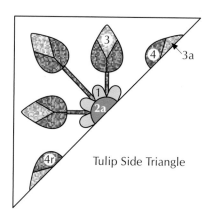

Tulip Side Triangle

1. Make a full-size paper pattern of the Tulip block, including all placement lines.
2. Fold the 12½" muslin squares in quarters and on the diagonals. Finger-press to crease the fold lines. Lay each square on the pattern, aligning the creases with the placement lines. Using a pencil, lightly trace the design onto the fabric.

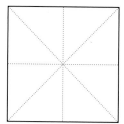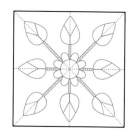

3. Trace the tulip pattern onto the gold squares and triangles.

4. Prepare appliqué pieces, referring to pages 81–84.

5. Place pieces 4 and 4 reversed right sides together. Sew them together on the short, straight line, starting and stopping at the seam intersections; do not stitch into the seam allowances. Press the seam allowance open.

Adding the Appliqués
Stems, Buds, and Flowers

1. Fold each green bias strip in half lengthwise, wrong sides together. Using a 1/4"-wide seam allowance, stitch along the long edges. The distance from the fold to the stitching line should measure the finished stem width plus one or two threads.

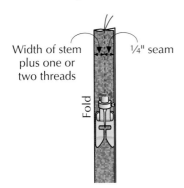

Width of stem plus one or two threads

1/4" seam

Fold

2. To make a 1/4"-wide finished stem, trim the seam allowance of a bias strip to 1/8". Place the seam on the left stem placement line of a background square as shown. Stitch the stem to the background along the placement line.

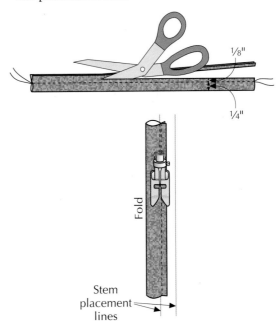

1/8"

1/4"

Fold

Stem placement lines

3. Fold the stem over and appliqué it to the background, making sure the fold of the stem covers the other placement line.

Stem placement lines

4. Position and appliqué the petals and then the circles onto the background squares.

5. Appliqué the petals and circles onto the sashing squares and triangles.

Sashing Units

Circles

One of the oldest and best ways to get smooth-edged circles is the paper-patch method.

1. Trace the template onto heavy paper and cut it out. Trace around the paper circle onto fabric, and then cut out the fabric circle, adding a ¼"-wide seam allowance.
2. With a single, knotted thread, sew a running stitch around the edge of the fabric circle.

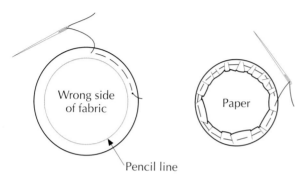

Wrong side of fabric

Paper

Pencil line

3. Place the paper template on the wrong side of the fabric circle. Pull the thread taut around the paper. Press with the paper inside.
4. Remove the paper and appliqué, or appliqué first, and then slit the background fabric and remove the paper with tweezers.

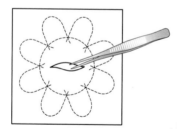

Outer Borders

1. Trace the border patterns from the pullout onto tissue paper, making a complete pattern for half the outer border.
2. Fold each outer border strip in half crosswise, and finger-press the fold.
3. Place the fold of an outer border strip on the pattern at the center line. Trace the design lightly onto the border strip with a sharp pencil. Reverse the pattern and trace it onto the other half of the strip. Repeat with the remaining outer border strips.

Fold

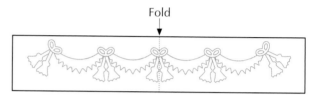

4. Position the inner swags and bows on the border strips and appliqué in place. Leave the corner bow, swags, and tassels to appliqué after the border has been attached to the quilt.

To reverse-appliqué the bows:

Trace the outlines of the bow openings onto the right side of the fabric bows with a light pencil. With sharply pointed scissors, carefully cut through the bow fabric only. Cut away the middle of the opening, leaving a ¼"-wide seam allowance. Clip the edges of the fabric almost to the seam line. Turn under the edges and stitch them to the background.

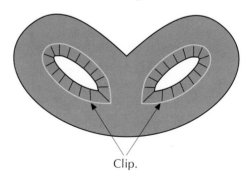

Clip.

Assembling the Quilt Top

1. Arrange the blocks, triangles, sashing strips, and sashing squares as shown.
2. Join the sashing squares and sashing strips. Press the seam allowances toward the sashing squares.

3. Join the Tulip blocks and sashing in diagonal rows. Press the seam allowances toward the sashing.

4. Join the rows, carefully matching the seams.

Adding the Inner Border

1. Sew together 11 green and 10 muslin piece 8. Add a green piece 9 to each end of the strip. Make 4 of row 1.

2. Sew together 10 green and 11 muslin piece 8. Add muslin piece 9 to each end of the strip. Make 4 of row 2.

3. Pin each row 1 to a row 2, aligning the points of the muslin triangles with the points of the green triangles. Pin at each point and ease or stretch to fit as necessary. Sew the rows together.

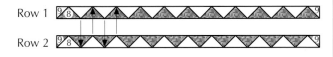

4. Sew inner border strips to opposite sides of the quilt top.

5. Add 1 Flower block to each end of the remaining pieced borders. Sew the borders to the top and bottom of the quilt top.

Adding the Outer Border

1. Mark the center of each side of the quilt top and of each outer border strip. Pin border strips to opposite sides of the quilt top, matching the center marks and ends and easing as necessary. Sew the border strips to the quilt top, pressing the seam allowances toward the borders. "Encouraging" the *quilt top* to fit the border, rather than easing or stretching the border, will help your quilt to finish square and flat.

2. Repeat for the top and bottom borders.

3. Position and appliqué the corner swags and bows.

Finishing

For detailed finishing instructions, refer to pages 85–87.

1. Using the patterns on the pullout, mark the quilting design on the quilt top.

2. Layer the quilt top with batting and backing; baste. Quilt on the marked lines and outline quilt each appliqué.

3. Bind and label your quilt.

Holiday Berry Baskets

By Mary Ellen Von Holt

Holiday Berry Baskets by Mary Ellen Von Holt, 1996, Marietta, Georgia, 30" x 30".

MARY ELLEN HAS BEEN QUILTING FOR ALMOST TWENTY YEARS AND LOVES ALL PHASES OF QUILTMAKING. SHE AND PARTNERS ALICE BERG AND SYLVIA JOHNSON COMBINE THEIR TALENTS TO PRODUCE LITTLE QUILTS PATTERNS, KITS, AND ACCESSORIES, WHICH ARE SOLD WORLDWIDE. LITTLE QUILTS ALSO DESIGNS A LINE OF FABRICS.

AS A QUILT DESIGNER AND QUILT-MAKER, MARY ELLEN PUTS HER ART AND ADVERTISING BACKGROUND TO GOOD USE. TRADITIONAL SCRAP QUILTS AND MULTI-FABRIC WALL HANGINGS ARE HER SPECIALTIES. SHE ALSO HAS FUN WITH RUG HOOKING.

MARY ELLEN LOVES HUNTING FOR ANTIQUE QUILT BLOCKS AT QUILT SHOWS AND FLEA MARKETS, AND HER PROJECT IN *QUILTED FOR CHRISTMAS, BOOK II* WAS A WALL HANGING MADE FROM ANTIQUE TREE BLOCKS. THE ANTIQUE BASKET BLOCKS THAT WERE THE INSPIRATION FOR THIS HOLIDAY TABLE TOPPER OR WALL HANGING ALSO CAME FROM A QUILT-SHOW SALE.

REPRODUCTION FABRICS, WHICH ARE BECOMING WIDELY AVAILABLE, HELPED IN COMBINING THE OLD WITH THE NEW FOR A FUN PROJECT. THE CREAM-PRINT BORDER COMPLEMENTED THE AGED MUSLIN, AND THE RED PRINT FOR THE SAWTOOTH BORDER ACCENTED THE RED SOLID ANTIQUE BASKET BLOCKS. SCRAPS OF RED MADE INTO YO-YOS ADDED A NICE FINISHING TOUCH AND COVERED PIECING IRREGULARITIES IN THE ANTIQUE BLOCKS.

THIS QUILT MAKES A NICE CENTERPIECE FOR A HOLIDAY TABLE, AS IT CAN BE VIEWED FROM ANY DIRECTION.

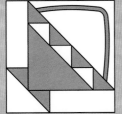

Quilt Size: 30" x 30"
Finished Block Size: 8¾" x 8¾"

Materials: 42"-wide fabric

¼ yd. red solid for baskets and handles

¼ yd. muslin for basket backgrounds

⅛ yd. gold print for inner sashing strip

⅛ yd. total assorted green prints for
leaves and sashing cornerstones

⅔ yd. cream print for inner border
and Sawtooth border

⅓ yd. red print for Sawtooth border and binding

⅛ yd. total assorted red prints for Yo-yo berries

34" x 34" square of backing fabric

34" x 34" square of thin batting

¼ yd. paper-backed fusible web

Black embroidery floss

Cutting

Use the templates on page 91.

From the red solid, cut:

2 squares, each 6⅛" x 6⅛"; cut each square in half once diagonally to make 4 triangles (A)

12 squares, each 2⅝" x 2⅝"; cut each square in half once diagonally to make 24 triangles (B)

4 strips on the bias, each 1½" x 12½", for basket handles

From the muslin, cut:

6 squares, each 2⅝" x 2⅝"; cut each square in half once diagonally to make 12 triangles (B)

2 squares, each 7⅞" x 7⅞"; cut each square in half once diagonally to make 4 (C)

2 squares, each 4⅜" x 4⅜"; cut each square in half once diagonally to make 4 triangles (D)

8 strips, each 2¼" x 5¾" (E)

From the gold print, cut:

4 strips, each 1¼" x 18", for sashing

From the assorted green prints, cut:

4 squares, each 1¼" x 1¼", for sashing corner-stones

From the cream print, cut:

2 strips, each 4½" x 19½", for side inner borders

2 strips, each 4½" x 27½", for top and bottom inner borders

72 squares, each 2" x 2", for Sawtooth border

2 squares, each 2⅜" x 2⅜"; cut each square in half once diagonally to make 4 triangles for Sawtooth border

From the red print for the border and binding, cut:

4 strips, each 1¼" x 40", for binding

36 strips, each 2" x 3½", for Sawtooth border

2 squares, each 2⅜" x 2⅜"; cut each square in half once diagonally to make 4 triangles for Sawtooth border

From the assorted red prints, cut:

28 Template 2 for Yo-yos

Making the Basket Blocks

To help with accurate stitching of the red and muslin B triangles, make a plastic version of Template 3 on page 91; include the seam allowance, but cut away two corners as indicated on the template. Use the template to trim the corners of the B triangles.

1. Join 3 muslin triangles (B), and 4 red triangles (B) into a strip as shown.

2. Carefully press over ½" of each long edge of a red bias strip, wrong sides together, to make a ½"-wide strip.

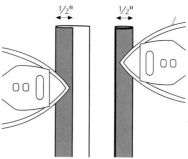

3. Pin the bias strip in a soft curve on a muslin triangle (C), with the ends at least ¾" from the corners. Baste, and then appliqué the basket handle to the muslin.

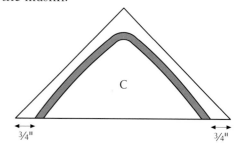

4. Assemble the Basket block as shown.

5. Sew the 4 Basket blocks together.

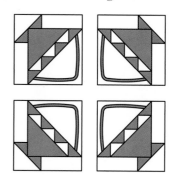

Adding Sashing and Borders

1. Sew a 1¼" x 18" gold strip to opposite sides of the quilt top. Press the seam allowances toward the gold strips.
2. Sew a 1¼" green square to each end of the remaining 2 gold strips, and then sew the strips to the top and bottom of the quilt top.
3. Sew one 4½" x 19½" cream strip each to the sides of the quilt top. Press the seam allowances outward. Sew the 4½" x 27½" strips to the top and bottom of the quilt top and press.

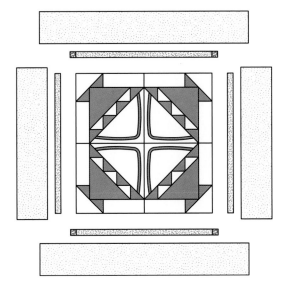

4. For each Sawtooth unit, draw diagonal lines on the backs of two 2" cream squares. Place 1 square on one end of a red print 2" x 3½" rectangle, right sides together. Stitch on the drawn line. Trim the *cream square only* to ¼" from the sewing line. Fold up and press.

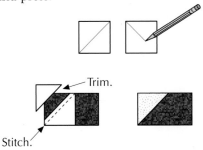

Trim.

Stitch.

5. Place the other cream square on the other end of the Sawtooth unit, stitch on the drawn line, and then trim and press as before.

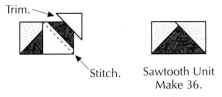

Trim.

Stitch.

Sawtooth Unit
Make 36.

6. Make 4 strips of 9 Sawtooth units each.

7. Sew 1 Sawtooth strip to each side of the quilt top.
8. Join the cream and red print triangles to make two-color squares. Stitch 1 square to each end of the remaining Sawtooth strips, and then add the strips to the top and bottom of the quilt top.

Adding the Appliqués

Holly Leaves

1. Following the manufacturer's directions, apply fusible web to the wrong side of the assorted green prints.
2. Using template 1 on page 91, cut out 8 holly leaves and 8 reversed.
3. Fuse 2 leaves to each Basket block, and 2 at each corner of the inner border as shown in the quilt diagram.

Hollyberry Yo-yos

1. Turn a ⅛" hem to the wrong side of each red circle, and use a double thread or a quilting thread to make a running stitch close to the fold.
2. After stitching around the circle, pull the thread to gather, making a small knot to secure. Feed the needle through the fold and out before cutting the thread. This will hide the end of the thread.
3. Flatten each gathered circle with your fingers. After the quilt has been quilted, attach the Yo-yos as shown in the photo.

Make 28.

Finishing

For detailed finishing instructions, refer to pages 85–87.
1. Mark the quilt top with desired quilting pattern.
2. Layer the quilt top with the batting and backing; baste. Quilt on the marked lines.
3. Bind and label your quilt.

Stocking Stuffers

by Eileen Westfall

Stocking Stuffers *by Eileen Westfall, September 1996,*
Walnut Creek, California, 31" x 39", quilted by Katherine Bilton.

A LOVER OF QUILTS SINCE SHE WAS A CHILD AND A DESIGNER FOR MORE THAN TWENTY YEARS, EILEEN WESTFALL IS THE AUTHOR OF NUMEROUS MAGAZINE ARTICLES AND EIGHT BOOKS ON QUILTING, INCLUDING *BASIC BEAUTIES: EASY QUILTS FOR BEGINNERS* AND *QUILTS SAY IT BEST*, PUBLISHED BY THAT PATCHWORK PLACE. SHE LIVES WITH HER HUSBAND, JOHN, SON DAMIAN, AND THEIR COCKER SPANIEL, JOSEY, IN A QUILT-FILLED HOUSE IN WALNUT CREEK, CALIFORNIA.

EILEEN IS ONE OF THOSE QUILTMAKERS WHO CAN'T TURN OFF THE IDEAS. A SHOW AND DINNER WITH OTHER QUILT DESIGNERS WAS NUTRITION FOR THE IDEA CENTER OF HER BRAIN. HER MIND WAS STIRRING WITH CHRISTMAS IDEAS, AND THIS PATTERN IS THE RESULT.

FOUR FUN STOCKINGS ARE THE FOCUS OF THIS QUILT. EACH STOCKING SPORTS A NINE PATCH BLOCK IN ITS CENTER AND FEATURES A CUDDLY TOY STICKING OUT OF ITS TOP. A DOLL, A TEDDY BEAR, A GINGERBREAD MAN, AND A SNOWMAN ARE THE STOCKING STUFFERS. EACH FIGURE HOLDS A TREAT IN ITS HAND, MAKING A FESTIVE CHRISTMAS QUILT FOR KIDS OF ALL AGES.

Quilt Size: 31" x 39"

Materials: 42"-wide fabric

½ yd. white-and-red print

¼ yd. *each* red print #1 and red print #2

⅓ yd. red print #3

¾ yd. blue print #1

¼ yd. blue print #2

¼ yd. *each* tan print and tan solid

½ yd. white-and-green print

¼ yd. medium green print

¼ yd. *each* dark green print #1 and dark green print #2

⅛ yd. white

Scrap of brown

Scrap of pink

35" x 43" piece of batting

1¼ yds. for backing and binding

Embroidery thread: brown, red, dark, green, pink, blue, black, and white

Embellishments: 1 small black ball button, 1 small red heart button, 1 small bell, ⅓ yd. of 1/16"-wide green satin ribbon

Cutting

Use the templates on pages 92–94.

From the white-and-red print, cut:
2 rectangles, 11½" x 15½" (A)
4 squares, each 1½" x 1½" (E)
8 squares, each 1⅞" x 1⅞"; cut each square once
diagonally to make 16 half-square triangles (G)

From the assorted red prints, cut:
2 stockings
Snowman scarf 3–5
15 squares, each 1½" x 1½" (E)
2 squares, each 1⅞" x 1⅞"; cut each square once
diagonally to make 4 half-square triangles (G)
8 squares, each 2" x 2" (D)
2 squares, each 4¼" x 4¼"; cut each square
twice diagonally to make 8 quarter-square
triangles (F)
1 lollipop for doll
1 bear paw and 1 reversed

From the assorted blue prints, cut:
6 strips, each 3½" x 15½"(C)
6 strips, each 3½" x 11½" (B)
5 squares, each 1½" x 1½"(E)
1 hat for doll
2 hat brims for doll

From the tan print, cut:
7 squares, each 1½" x 1½" (E)
4 strips, each ½" x 6", for stocking tops
4 stocking heels
4 stocking toes
1 broom for snowman

From the tan solid, cut:
1 teddy bear
1 gingerbread man
1 outer ear for teddy bear and 1 reversed

From the white-and-green print, cut:
2 rectangles, 11½" x 15½" (A)
4 squares, each 1½" x 1½" (E)
4 squares, each 1⅞" x 1⅞"; cut each square once
diagonally to make 8 half-square triangles (G)

From the medium green print, cut:
11 squares, each 1½" x 1½"
8 squares, each 2" x 2" (D)
2 squares, each 4¼" x 4¼"; cut each square
twice diagonally to make 8 quarter-square
triangles (F)
Tie 4–6 for teddy bear
1 doll dress

From the assorted dark green prints, cut:
2 stockings
6 squares, each 1⅞" x 1⅞"; cut each square once
diagonally to make 12 half-square triangles (G)
4 strips, each 2½" x 42", for binding

From the white, cut:
1 snowman
1 doll collar and 1 reversed

From the brown scrap, cut:
1 hat for snowman

From the pink scrap, cut:
1 doll face
2 doll hands
1 teddy bear inner ear and 1 reversed

Making the Stocking Blocks

Refer to pages 81–84 for detailed appliqué instructions. Use your favorite method to prepare the appliqué pieces.

1. Fold the ½" x 6" tan print strips in half lengthwise and stitch one to the top of each stocking.

2. Using 1½" squares (E) and 1⅞" half-square triangles (G), make the patchwork blocks for the stockings as shown. Refer to the photo on page 30 for fabric placement.

Monkey Wrench
Block

Friendship Star
Block

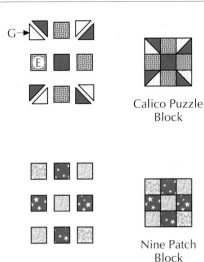

Calico Puzzle
Block

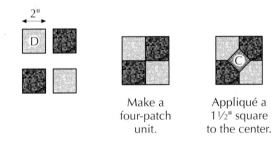

Nine Patch
Block

3. Appliqué the character pieces to each piece A in numerical order. To each stocking, sew a stocking toe, appliqué a heel, and then appliqué each stocking to a background block. Appliqué a patchwork block to each stocking. Embroider as indicated on the patterns. Use 1 strand of embroidery thread for delicate details and 3 strands for heavier lines.

Making the Border Blocks

Using 2" squares, 4¹⁄₄" quarter-square triangles, and 1¹⁄₂" squares, make the border blocks as shown.

Make a
four-patch
unit.

Appliqué a
1¹⁄₂" square
to the center.

Bow Tie Block
Make 4.

Quarter-Square
Triangle Block
Make 3.

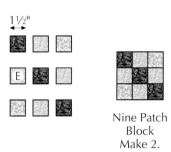

Nine Patch
Block
Make 2.

Assembling the Quilt Top

Arrange the blocks and strips as shown. Sew them into horizontal rows, and then sew the rows together.

Finishing

For detailed finishing instructions, refer to pages 85–87.
1. Layer the backing, batting, and quilt top; baste.
2. Quilt in-the-ditch to outline blocks, stockings, and figures, or quilt as desired.
3. Bind the quilt, and then add a sleeve and label.

33

Folk-Art Christmas Banner

By Tonee White

**Folk-Art
Christmas Banner**
*by Tonee White,
1995, Irvine, California, 72" x 16".*

TONEE WHITE

Tonee began quilting seven years ago as a hobby. Four years later it had become her full-time profession and consuming passion. Tonee's main goal has been to develop techniques to make quilting easier and less intimidating. Her Appliquilt® technique does just that, and she has published four Appliquilt books with That Patchwork Place.

Tonee continues to develop her skills in other areas, such as sashiko and a new needleturn Appliquilt method used in this Christmas project. She teaches and lectures extensively and continues to develop new techniques and designs.

Home is Irvine, California, where she lives happily with her husband, Bob, and three of her seven children. She delights in four grandchildren who live nearby.

Brightly colored birds, stars, and a Christmas wreath spell Christmas in the best folk-art tradition. This banner was designed to be used as a holiday valance in Tonee's home. You can create a holiday valance to fit your draperies simply by adding or eliminating Churn Dash blocks.

Quilt Size: 72" x 16"
Finished Block Size: 9" x 9"

Materials: 42"-wide fabric

1 yd. white solid for blocks and borders

1/2 yd. gold print for blocks, stars, and heart

3/4 yd. red print for outer border and binding

1/2 yd. green print for vine and leaves

Scraps of assorted greens for wreath

1/8 yd. red solid for bow

Scraps of assorted reds for bow knot, dots, and birds

Scraps of assorted blues for birds

1 1/4 yds. for backing

80" x 24" piece of batting

Cutting

Use the templates on pages 96–97.

From the white solid, cut:

6 squares, each 3½" x 3½"

12 squares, each 3⅞" x 3⅞"; cut each square in half once diagonally to make 24 triangles

6 strips, each 2" x 42", for Churn Dash blocks and inner borders

7 rectangles, each 2½" x 9½"

3 strips, each 2½" x 42", for outer borders

From the gold print, cut:

12 squares, each 3⅞" x 3⅞"; cut each square in half once diagonally to make 24 triangles

2 strips, each 2" x 42", for Churn Dash blocks

3 Stars

1 Heart

From the red print, cut:

7 strips, each 2½" x 42", for outer borders and binding

From the green print, cut:

2 bias strips, each 1½" x 36", for vines

52 Leaf C

From the scraps of assorted greens, cut:

35 Leaf A–C in any combination

Piecing the Churn Dash Blocks

1. Sew 1 gold and 1 white triangle together to form a square. Press the seam allowance toward the gold fabric. Make 24 squares.

2. Sew each gold 2" x 42" strip to a white strip of the same size. Press the seam allowance toward the gold fabric. Make 2 strip units.

3. Crosscut the units into a total of 24 segments, each 3½" wide.

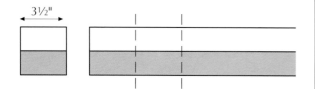

4. Join the pieces as shown to complete the Churn Dash blocks. Make 6 blocks.

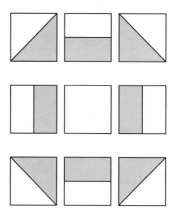

Assembling the Quilt Top

1. Sew the Churn Dash blocks together to form a row, placing white 2½" x 9½" rectangles between each block and at each end. Press the seam allowances toward the blocks. Using the 2" x 42" white strips, piece two 2" x 68½" strips. Sew them to the top and bottom of the row.

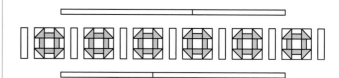

2. Sew 3 red and 3 white 2½"-wide strips together lengthwise. Press the seam allowances toward the red strips. Crosscut the strip unit into 14 segments, each 2½" wide.

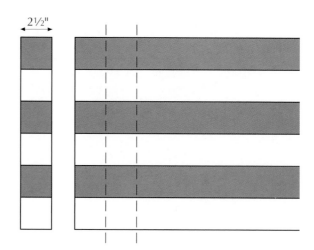

4. Sew a pieced segment to each end of the banner.

5. Join 6 pieced segments end to end, alternating red and white squares. Press the seam allowances toward the red squares. Sew the strip to the top of the banner. Repeat for the bottom.

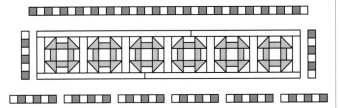

Finishing

For detailed finishing instructions, refer to pages 85–87.

1. Layer the quilt top with batting and backing. Baste.
2. Using matching thread, quilt the banner as shown.

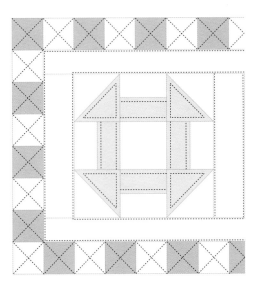

3. Bind the edges with the 2¹/₂"-wide red strips.

Adding the Appliqués

For detailed appliqué instructions, refer to pages 81–84.

Refer to the color photo and to the quilt diagram for placement of appliqué motifs. You appliqué through all the layers, quilting at the same time.

1. Referring to "Stems, Buds, and Flowers" on page 23, use the green bias strips to make vines.
2. Pin the vines in place on the banner, and then appliqué them, stitching through all layers.
3. Draw a circle 7" in diameter in the center of the banner. Arrange the leaves in a wreath configuration, overlapping edges and using the drawn circle as a guide. Pin the leaves in place and appliqué through all layers. Sew a running stitch down the center of each leaf to create a vein.
4. Appliqué the birds and bow in place, following the numerical order for each motif.
5. Appliqué 52 additional Leaf C to the vine.
6. Appliqué the stars and dots as desired.
7. Sign and date your quilt.

Pioneer Braid Stocking

By Deborah J. Moffett-Hall

Pioneer Braid Stocking
by Deborah J. Moffett-Hall,
1996, Hatfield, Pennsylvania, 8″ x 19″.

DEBORAH HAS BEEN QUILTING SINCE 1987, WHEN SHE MADE A BABY QUILT FOR HER FIRST CHILD. AFTER PIECING A FEW PATTERNS FROM BOOKS AND MAGAZINES, DEB BEGAN TO DESIGN AND DRAFT HER OWN PATTERNS. HER FIRST PUBLISHED PATTERN APPEARED IN THE 1989 SPRING ISSUE OF *QUILT* MAGAZINE. SHE IS CURRENTLY SPECIAL PROJECTS EDITOR FOR *QUILT* AND SEVERAL OTHER HARRIS PUBLICATIONS. DEBORAH'S DESIGNS HAVE BEEN FEATURED IN *QUILTED FOR CHRISTMAS BOOKS I & II*, AS WELL AS IN HER OWN BOOK, *TRADITIONAL BLOCKS MEET APPLIQUÉ*, ALL FROM THAT PATCHWORK PLACE.

DEBORAH LIVES IN HATFIELD, PENNSYLVANIA, WITH HER HUSBAND, SCOTT, AND DAUGHTER MICHELLE AND BABY DANIEL. DEB COLLECTS FAT QUARTERS AND FAT EIGHTHS OF HOMESPUN PLAIDS AND STRIPES FROM THE QUILTING SHOWS SHE ATTENDS THROUGHOUT THE YEAR. THE STACK OF REDS AND GREENS THREATENED TO TOPPLE, SO SHE DECIDED TO USE A FEW IN THIS PROJECT BEFORE THEY FELL ON HER HEAD. THIS STOCKING IS LARGE ENOUGH TO REALLY STUFF WITH HOLIDAY TREATS AND GIFTS!

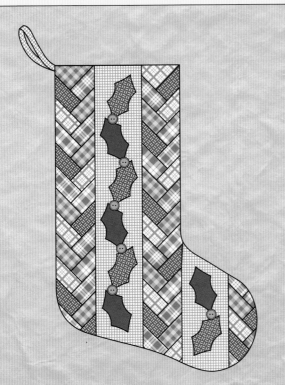

Project Size: 8" x 19"

Materials: 42"-wide fabric

2 green fat quarters (18" x 22") for holly

8 or more fat eighths (9" x 10½") of red and green prints or plaids

⅛ yd. light plaid

⅞ yd. light stripe for stocking back, lining, and hanging loop

6 flat, red ⅝" buttons

12" x 23" rectangle of thin batting

Cutting

Use the templates on the pullout.

From each green fat quarter, cut:
  4 Leaf templates for a total of 8 leaves
From 1 fat eighth, cut:
  3 squares, each 2½" x 2½", for starter squares
From the remaining fat eighths and the remaining green, cut:
  64 strips, each 1½" x 3¼", for braid strips
From the light stripe or plaid, cut:
  1 strip, 3½" x 9"
  1 strip, 3½" x 20"
From the lining fabric, cut:
  1 stocking pattern and 2 reversed
  1 strip, 1" x 6½", for hanging loop

Assembling the Stocking Front

1. Stitch one 1½" x 3¼" braid strip to the edge of a 2½" starter square as shown. Press the seam allowance toward the braid segment.

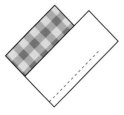 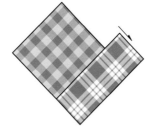

2. Add another braid strip as shown, and press the seam allowance toward the braid segment.

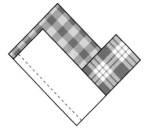 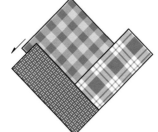

3. Continue adding braid strips, alternating sides and colors, until the strip has a total of 25 braid segments.

4. Make another braid band with 25 strips and a third band with 11 strips.

5. Trim the braid bands as shown to measure 3" wide; trim the starter square to square up the top of each band.

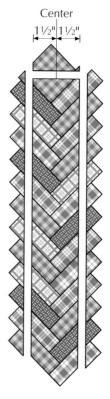

6. Using the Stocking pattern as a placement guide, sew together the braid bands and the 3½"-wide light strips. Press the seam allowances toward the light strips.

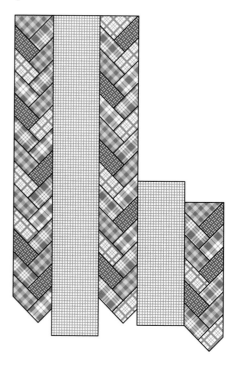

7. Refer to the stocking pattern to position the holly leaves. Using the appliqué method of your choice, stitch the leaves to the stocking.

8. Place the stocking pattern over the completed stocking front and trace; then cut along the traced lines.

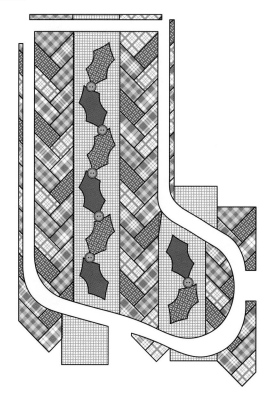

Finishing the Stocking

1. Cut a piece of batting slightly larger on all sides than the stocking pattern. Place the completed and pressed stocking front right side up on the batting, and pin or baste the layers together.

2. By machine or by hand, quilt along the seam lines and around the holly leaves. Trim the excess batting, and sew the buttons in place.

3. Press the 1" x 6½" strip of lining fabric in half lengthwise. Open the strip, and then fold the long edges so they meet the center crease; press. Fold the strip in half again to enclose the raw edges; press. Stitch the folded edges together to make a hanging loop.

Fold edges to the center.

Stitch folded edges together.

4. Place the stocking front and back right sides together, matching the edges. Pin the hanging loop between the pieces, near the top and pointing slightly toward the toe. Using a ¼"-wide seam allowance, stitch around the raw edges of the stocking, leaving the top edge unsewn; clip curves. Turn the stocking right side out and press. Repeat with the lining pieces. Leave the lining wrong side out.

5. Insert the stocking into the lining; then align and pin the top edges, right sides together. Using a ½"-wide seam allowance, sew around the top edge, leaving a 3"- to 4"-wide opening.

6. Pull the stocking out through the opening, and push the lining into the stocking. Hand stitch the opening closed.

Northern Stars

By Roxanne Carter

Northern Stars by Roxanne Carter, 1996, Mukilteo, Washington, 42" x 42".

☙ ROXANNE CARTER ❧

(See page 6 for author background.)

ROXANNE DESIGNED "NORTHERN STARS" AS A MYS-
TERY QUILT FOR A CLASS. SHE WANTED A QUILT MADE OF
SIMPLE UNITS THAT WENT TOGETHER IN SUCH A WAY THAT
THE STUDENTS COULD NOT GUESS WHAT THEY WERE
MAKING UNTIL THE END. NOTICE THAT IF THE LARGE
TRIANGLES IN THE UNITS ARE MADE WITH THE MEDIUM FAB-
RIC INSTEAD OF THE DARK FABRIC, YOU SEE STARS INSTEAD
OF PINWHEELS.

Quilt Size: 42" x 42"

Materials: 42"-wide fabric

1 yd. Christmas print

3/4 yd. dark red

1/2 yd. medium green

3/4 yd. background print

1/2 yd. cream

Cutting

Fabric	Piece	Cut
Christmas print	A	9 squares, each 3½" x 3½"
	D	12 squares, each 2⅝" x 2⅝"
	Borders	4 strips, each 4" x 42"
Dark red	B	18 squares, each 3⅞" x 3⅞"; cut each square once diagonally to make 36 triangles
	D	12 squares, each 2⅝" x 2⅝"
Medium green	E	11 squares, each 4¼" x 4¼"; cut each square twice diagonally to make 44 triangles
	D	8 squares, each 2⅝" x 2⅝"
Background print	C	2 squares, each 7¼" x 7¼"; cut each square twice diagonally to make 8 triangles
	F	2 squares, each 4¾" x 4¾"
	D	12 squares, each 2⅝" x 2⅝"
	E	3 squares, each 4¼" x 4¼"; cut each square twice diagonally to make 12 triangles
	B	4 squares, each 3⅞" x 3⅞"; cut each square once diagonally to make 8 triangles
Cream	B	20 squares, each 3⅞" x 3⅞"; cut each square once diagonally to make 40 triangles
	E	18 squares, each 4¼" x 4¼"; cut each square twice diagonally to make 72 triangles

Constructing the Units

Unit 1
Sew green E triangles to opposite sides of background print D squares as shown. Add red B triangles to the sides. Make 12 units.

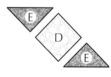

Unit 2
Sew together green and background print E triangles. Add a red B triangle. Make 12 units.

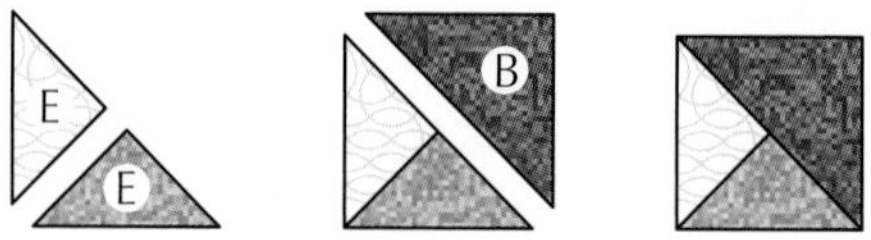

Unit 3
Sew together background print and cream B triangles. Make 8 units.

Unit 4

Sew 1 red B triangle to each short side of a background print C triangle. Make 8 units.

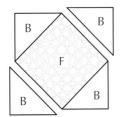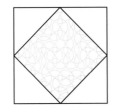

Unit 5

1. Sew cream B triangles to opposite sides of a background-print square F. Press the seam allowances toward the triangles.
2. Sew cream B triangles to the other 2 sides of the unit. Make 4 units.

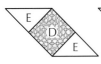

Unit 6

Sew cream E triangles to opposite sides of each D square as shown.

Make 12 with Christmas print. Make 12 with red. Make 8 with green.

Unit 7

Sew green E triangles to background print E triangles. Make 8 units.

Assembling the Quilt Top

1. Assemble units 6 and 7 as shown. Make 4 border strips.

2. Arrange the units as shown. Sew the units into rows, and then sew the rows together.

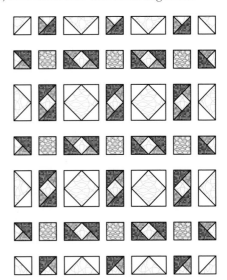

3. Sew pieced border strips to opposite sides of the quilt top. Sew a Unit 3 block to each end of the remaining border strips, and then sew the strips to the top and bottom of the quilt top.

4. Sew the 4"-wide Christmas print strips to the quilt top, referring to "Mitered-Corner Borders" on pages 84–85.

Finishing

For detailed finishing instructions, refer to pages 85–87.
1. Mark the quilt top with desired quilting pattern.
2. Layer the quilt top with batting and backing; baste.
3. Quilt on the marked lines.
4. Add a hanging sleeve if desired.
5. Bind and label your quilt.

Radiant Star Tree Skirt

By Gretchen Kluth Hudock

Radiant Star Tree Skirt by Gretchen Kluth Hudock, August 1996, Slinger, Wisconsin, 45" x 45".

GRETCHEN KLUTH HUDOCK

GRETCHEN DEVELOPED AN INTEREST IN TEXTILE ART WHILE ATTENDING THE UNIVERSITY OF WISCONSIN–MADISON, WHERE SHE GRADUATED WITH RELATED ART AND TEXTILES AND CLOTHING DEGREES. GRETCHEN BEGAN QUILTING IN 1984, WATCHING TELEVISION QUILTING PROGRAMS WHEN HER CHILDREN, JOHN AND ELIZABETH, WERE SMALL. GRETCHEN BEGAN DESIGNING PATTERNS IN 1989 AND PUBLISHING IN 1992. SHE LIVES IN SLINGER, WISCONSIN, WITH HER TWO CHILDREN AND HER HUSBAND, RICH.

CHRISTMAS HAS BECOME A SPECIALTY OF GRETCHEN'S. HER HOLIDAY DESIGNS HAVE BEEN PUBLISHED BY THAT PATCHWORK PLACE AND RODALE PRESS, AND BY COUNTRY HANDCRAFTS AND QUILT CRAFT MAGAZINES. IN ADDITION, GRETCHEN'S SELF-PUBLISHED LINE OF PATTERNS HAS A HOLIDAY FOCUS. SHE ENJOYS DESIGNING PROJECTS THAT MAKE NICE GIFTS BUT DON'T TAKE HOURS TO MAKE. THIS IS GRETCHEN'S SEVENTH PUBLISHED TREE-SKIRT PATTERN. IF ONLY SHE HAD MORE CHRISTMAS TREES!

Skirt Size: 45" x 45"

Materials: 42"-wide fabric

$3/4$ yd. red print

$1 1/4$ yds. Christmas print

$1/2$ yd. light print #1

$1/2$ yd. light print #2

$1 2/3$ yds. for backing

54" x 54" piece of batting

Hunter Star Block

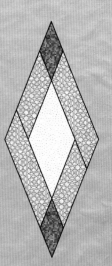

Diamond Block

Cutting

From the red print, cut:

8 strips, each 2¹/₂" x 42"; crosscut the strips into a total of 48 rectangles, each 2¹/₂" x 6". (Use the remaining fabric to cut bias strips for the tree-skirt center binding.)

From the Christmas print, cut:

2 strips, each 2¹/₂" x 42"

4 strips, each 2¹/₂" x 42"; crosscut the strips into a total of 16 rectangles, each 2¹/₂" x 10"

4 squares, each 8¹/₂" x 8¹/₂", cut each square once diagonally to make 8 triangles

4 strips, each 2¹/₂" x 42", for binding

From light print #1, cut:

1 strip, 3¹/₄" x 42"

4 strips, each 2¹/₂" x 42"; crosscut the strips into a total of 14 rectangles, each 2¹/₂" x 8¹/₄", and 2 rectangles, each 2¹/₂" x 8³/₄"

From light print #2, cut:

4 squares, each 8¹/₂" x 8¹/₂"; cut each square once diagonally to make 8 triangles

2 strips, each 1¹/₂" x 25", for open-edge binding

Making the Diamond Blocks

1. Sew a 2¹/₂" x 42" Christmas print strip to each side of the 3¹/₄"-wide light print #1 strip. Stagger the strips by 2¹/₂" as shown. Press the seam allowances toward the Christmas print strips.

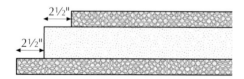

2. Crosscut the staggered strip unit, at a 45° angle, into 8 segments, each 3¹/₄" wide.

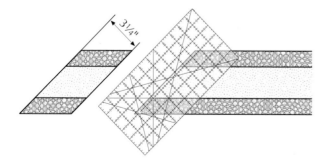

3. Sew a 2¹/₂" x 6" red rectangle to a 2¹/₂" x 10" Christmas print rectangle as shown. Stitch across the corner at a precise 45° angle; marking the stitching line with a pencil may help. Trim the corner ¹/₄" from the stitching line. Press the seam allowance toward the Christmas print. Make 16 pieced rectangles.

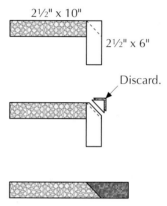

4. Sew 1 pieced rectangle to each long side of a strip-unit segment, matching seams. The rectangles will be longer than the strip-unit segments. Press the seam allowances away from the center. Trim the extensions even with the strip-unit segment. Make 8 diamonds.

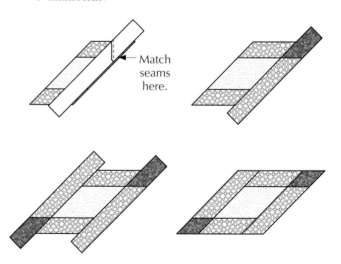

Making the Hunter Star Blocks

1. Sew the 2$\frac{1}{2}$" x 6" red rectangles to the light print #1 rectangles as shown. Mark a stitching line on each end of each red strip. Stitch on the line. Trim the seam allowance to $\frac{1}{4}$". Press half the units toward red and half toward light print #1. Make 14 strips using the 8$\frac{1}{4}$" rectangles and 2 strips using the 8$\frac{3}{4}$" rectangles. Set the long strips aside.

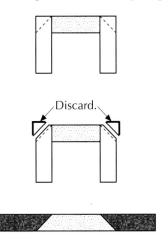

2. Stitch the short strips together in pairs, matching the seams.

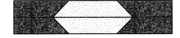

3. Sew Christmas print and light print #2 triangles to the long sides of the unit, centering the triangles on each side. Press the seam allowances toward the triangles.

4. Square the blocks to 10" x 10". If you place a large square ruler on the block, the seam lines of the corner diamonds should line up with the 2$\frac{1}{4}$" marks as shown.

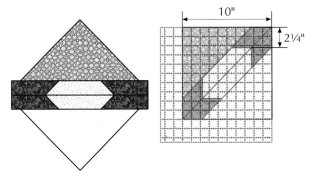

5. Sew the long strips together, and then sew Christmas print and light print #2 triangles to the sides. Square up the block to 10$\frac{1}{4}$" x 10$\frac{1}{4}$". Cut this block in half diagonally. These pieces are for the open edges of the tree skirt.

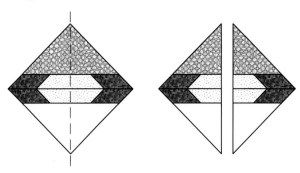

Assembling the Quilt Top

1. Stitch 2 diamonds together, starting and stopping at the $\frac{1}{4}$" seam intersections. Backstitch at each end. Repeat with the other diamonds to make 4 sections.

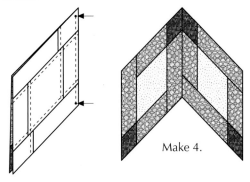

Make 4.

2. Arrange Hunter Star blocks and diamond sections as shown, and then sew them together in the order indicated.

3. Set in the Hunter Star blocks by first sewing 1 side of the block to 1 side of the adjacent diamond, stitching from seam intersection to outer edge. Remove from the sewing machine. Match the other side of the block with the adjacent diamond side, pushing the seam allowances out of the way, and stitching from seam intersection to outer edge.

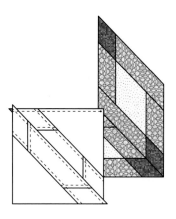

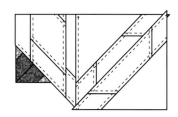

4. Arrange the remaining Hunter Star blocks and diamonds as shown, and sew them together in the order indicated. Sew the sections together on one side only, from the center to the outer edge.

Finishing

1. Cut the backing fabric lengthwise into 2 pieces, each 21" x 50", and 2 pieces, each 5" x 42". Sew the pieces together as shown, leaving an opening from the center to the outer edge

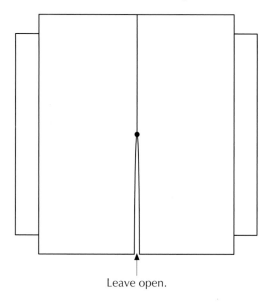

Leave open.

2. Layer the top with the batting and backing, matching the open edges. Quilt as desired. Gretchen suggests stitching in-the-ditch around the pieces and stipple quilting the triangles between the star points.

3. To cut out the center opening, draw a circle of the desired size on stiff paper or template plastic. Place it over the center of the skirt. Trace around the template, and then cut on the line.

4. Stitch a light print #2 binding strip to each open straight edge of the tree skirt. Fold each strip to the back and blindstitch to the backing.

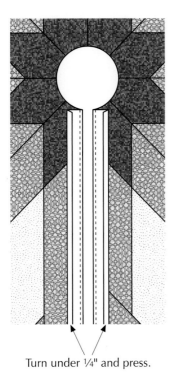

Turn under ¼" and press.

5. Cut 1½"-wide red bias strips and sew them together to make a strip that equals the circumference of the center opening plus 16". Fold one edge under ¼" and press.

6. Find the center of the strip and match it with the point on the circle opposite the opening. Pin the strip in place and stitch it to the front of the skirt, right sides together, using a ¼"-wide seam allowance.

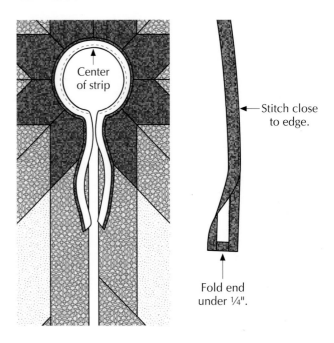

Center of strip

Stitch close to edge.

Fold end under ¼".

7. Bring the folded edge of the strip to the back, and then stitch it to the backing. Fold the raw edges of each tail in and stitch them together.

8. Sew together the 2½"-wide Christmas print strips to make 1 strip that equals the distance around the skirt plus a few inches (approximately 160").

9. Pin the binding strip to the front of the skirt, right sides together, aligning raw edges. Stitch the binding to the skirt using a ¼"-wide seam allowance. Fold the strip to the back; stitch it to the backing.

Heart and Home

By Retta Warehime

Heart and Home by Retta Warehime, 1996, Kennewick, Washington, 45" x 53".

It's been more than eighteen years since Retta pieced her first quilt. Since then, she has designed more than eighty original patterns and self-published many of them under the name of her company, Sew Cherished. Some of her other patterns have appeared in books and magazines.

Retta's typical day involves many hours of designing, piecing, and quilting. Each quilt is a labor of love that creates its own energy, so Retta never tires of the design process.

Retta enjoys all aspects of quiltmaking, but she is particularly intrigued by the process of piecing. Her primary focus is developing fast and easy rotary-cut patterns.

Recently, Retta has become hooked on flannel fabrics. "Heart and Home" blends her love of flannel with Star, House, and Log Cabin blocks. The Log Cabin block is a heartwarming base for any quilt, so the Log Cabin Hearts are special symbols of holiday love and warmth. Wrapping up in this cuddly quilt on a cold winter's night is certain to give you that "Heart and Home" feeling!

Quilt Size: 45" x 53"

Materials: 42"-wide fabric

The scrappier this quilt is, the better! Now is the time to dig through your scrap basket.
5 pieces, 1/8 yd. *each*, of green, blue, red, tan, cream, white, brown, and black

2/3 yd. tan for Heart and House blocks backgrounds

1/8 yd. green for trees

1/8 yd. brown for trunks

3/4 yd. red print for outer border

5/8 yd. green plaid for binding

2 2/3 yds. for backing

49" x 57" piece of batting

House Blocks

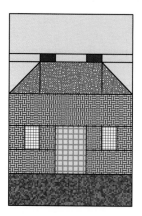

Cutting

Each house is a different color. Cutting instructions are for 1 House block. You need to make 3 blocks.

Piece	No. to Cut	Dimensions
Tan background	1	3" x 8½"
	1	2⅞" x 2⅞"
	3	1" x 2½"
Chimney	2	1" x 1½"
Roof	1	2½" x 4½"
	1	2⅞" x 2⅞"
House	1	2½" x 8½"
	2	2" x 3½"
	4	1½" x 2"
Window	2	1½" x 2"
Door	1	2½" x 3½"
Grass	1	2½" x 8½"

Assembly

1. Sew 1½" x 2" house pieces to opposite sides of a 1½" x 2" window piece. Sew this unit to the 2" x 3½" house piece. Make 2 window units.

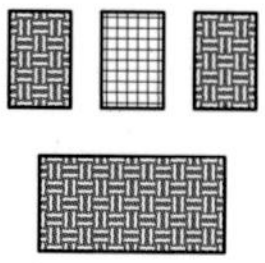

2. Sew a window unit to each side of the 2½" x 3½" door piece. Sew the 2½" x 8½" house piece to the top of this unit and the 2½" x 8½" grass piece to the bottom.

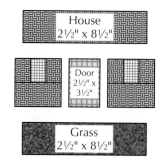

3. Place the 2⅞" background and roof squares right sides together. On the lighter piece, draw a diagonal line from corner to corner. Stitch ¼" from each side of this line.

4. Cut on the drawn line, open the unit, and press toward the background.

5. Sew 1 unit to each short side of the 2½" x 4½" roof piece.

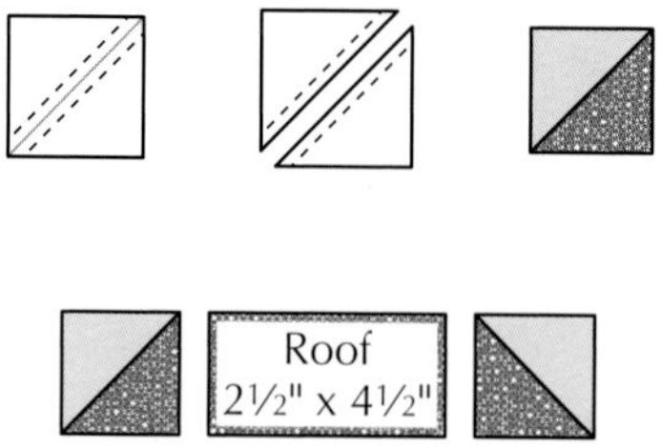

6. Sew 1" x 2½" background pieces and 1" x 1½" chimney pieces together as shown; then add the 3" x 8½" background piece to the top.

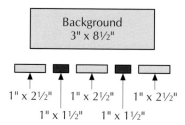

7. Join all the units to make the house. Press and set aside. The unfinished block should measure 8¹/₂" x 12¹/₂".

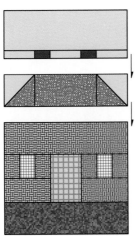

Tree Blocks

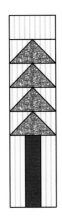

Cutting

Cutting instructions are for 1 Tree block. Make 6 blocks, varying the background fabrics.

Piece	No. to Cut	Dimensions
Cream background	1	2" x 3¹/₂"
	8	2" x 2"
	2	1¹/₂" x 5"
Tree	4	2" x 3¹/₂"
Trunk	1	1¹/₂" x 5"

Assembly

1. Place a 2" background square on an end of a 2" x 3¹/₂" tree piece, right sides together. Stitch from corner to corner, and then trim to a ¹/₄"-wide seam allowance. Open the unit and press the seam allowance toward the background.

2. Repeat with another 2" background square at the other end of the tree piece. Make 4 tree units.

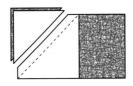

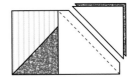

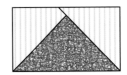

3. To make the trunk unit, sew a 1¹/₂" x 5" background piece to each side of the 1¹/₂" x 5" trunk piece.

4. Join all the tree units; then add the 2" x 3¹/₂" background piece to the top and the trunk unit to the bottom. The unfinished block should measure 3¹/₂" x 12¹/₂".

2 x 3¹/₂"

1¹/₂" x 5"

Heart Blocks

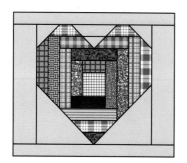

Cutting

*The cutting instructions are for all 3 Heart blocks.
The hearts are scrappy, with gold centers
and tan backgrounds.*

**To make the background pieces and Log Cabin
centers, cut strips of the following lengths:**

Piece	No. to Cut	Dimensions
Tan background	6	5½" x 5½"
	6	2½" x 10½"
	6	2½" x 2½"
	6	1½" x 14½"
	3	1½" x 4½"
	3	1½" x 2½"
Gold (piece #1)	3	2½" x 2½"

**To make the pieces for the Log Cabin hearts, cut one
1½" x 42" strip each from 16 different fabrics.
Crosscut them into strips of the following lengths.**

Piece	No. to Cut	Length
#2	3	2½"
#3, #4	6	3½"
#5, #6	6	4½"
#7	3	5½"
#8	3	5½"
#9	3	6½"
#10	6	3½"
#11, #12	6	7½"
#13	3	8½"
#14	6	4½"
#15, #16	6	9½"
#17	3	10½"

Assembly

1. Beginning with gold piece #1, build the Log Cabin
hearts. Add the pieces in numerical order, ending
with strip #9. Press away from the center after adding each strip.

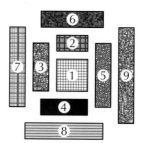

2. Place a strip #10 on a 1½" x 2½" background piece,
right sides together as shown. Stitch from corner
to corner, trim to a ¼"-wide seam allowance, and
press the unit open. Repeat with another strip #10
at the other end.

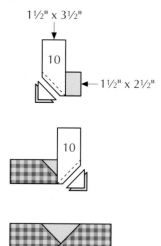

3. Place a strip #14 on the end of a 1½" x 4½" background strip, right sides together, as in step 2. Sew
from corner to corner, trim to a ¼"-wide seam allowance, and press the unit open. Repeat with
another strip #14 at the other end.

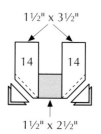

4. Continue assembling the block as shown. The unfinished block should measure 10½" x 10½".

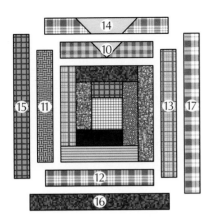

5. Sew a 2½" background square to each upper corner and a 5½" background square to each lower corner. Trim and press.

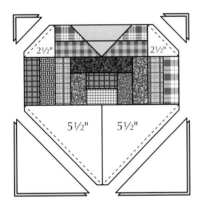

6. Add 2½" x 10½" background strips to each side of the Heart block and 1½" x 14½" strips to the top and bottom. The unfinished block should measure 14½" x 12½".

Star Blocks

Cutting

Cutting instructions are for 1 Star block. You need to make 20 blocks. Each star is scrappy, with a gold center.

Piece	No. to Cut	Dimensions
Background	4	1½" x 1½"
	4	1½ x 2½"
Star points	8	1½" x 1½"
Gold star center	1	2½" x 2½"

Assembly

1. Sew two 1½" star-point squares to each 1½" x 2½" background piece, referring to steps 1 and 2 of "Tree Blocks."

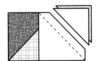

2. Assemble the star as shown. Press and set aside.

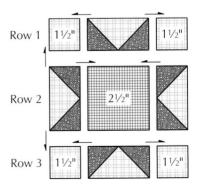

Log Cabin Blocks

Cutting

Cutting instructions are for 1 Log Cabin block. You need to make 16 blocks. Each Log Cabin block has a gold center and 12 scrappy logs.

From the gold fabric, cut one square, 1½" x 1½", for piece #1.

Cut one 1" x 42" strip each from 12 different light fabrics and 12 different dark fabrics, for a total of 24 strips. Cut the strips into the following lengths:

| Darks | | Lights | |
Piece	Length	Piece	Length
#2	1½"	#4	2"
#3	2"	#5	2½"
#6	2½"	#8	3"
#7	3"	#9	3½"
#10	3½"	#12	4"
#11	4"	#13	4½"

Assembly

Beginning with gold piece #1, build the Log Cabin block, adding light and dark strips in numerical order. Press the seam allowance away from the center after sewing each strip. The unfinished block should measure 4½" x 4½".

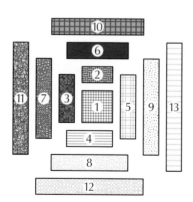

Assembling the Quilt

1. Sew a Tree block to each side of each House block.
2. Assemble the patchwork borders, positioning the lights and darks of the Log Cabin blocks as shown.

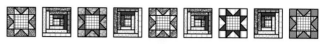

Border A
Make 2.

Border B
Make 2.

3. Sew the Heart blocks to the House blocks as shown.

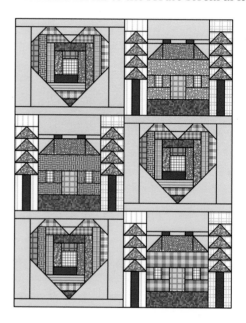

4. Sew 1 patchwork border A to each side of the quilt top and 1 row B each to the top and bottom. Be sure to position the lights and darks of the Log Cabins correctly.

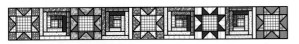

5. For the inner border, cut scraps into 1½"-wide strips of various lengths. Join the strips randomly, end to end, until you have a strip at least 200" long.

6. Measure through the center of the quilt vertically, and then cut 2 lengths of the pieced strip to match this length. Sew 1 strip to each side of the quilt.

7. Measure through the center of the quilt horizontally, and then cut 2 lengths of the inner border to match this length. Sew 1 strip each to the top and bottom of the quilt.

8. Cut 4 strips, each 6" x 42", from the red print for the outer border. Sew the outer border strips together end to end. Measure vertically through the center of the quilt, cut 2 strips to match this measurement, and then sew 1 strip to each side of the quilt. Measure horizontally through the center of the quilt, cut 2 strips to match this measurement, and then sew 1 strip each to the top and bottom of the quilt.

Finishing

For detailed finishing instructions, refer to pages 85–87.

1. Layer the quilt top with batting and backing; baste.
2. Quilt lines through the Log Cabin hearts. Quilt small hearts in the Star blocks, small grids on the roofs of the houses, and a curlicue of smoke coming out of each chimney.

3. Bind and label your quilt.

Father Christmas Sampler

By Barbara Nienow

Father Christmas Sampler *by Barbara Nienow, 1996, Jackson, Wisconsin, 52" x 58".*

A PERSON IS TRULY BLESSED WHEN SHE CAN EARN A WAGE DOING SOMETHING SHE LOVES. WHEN BARBARA MADE HER FIRST QUILT IN 1973, SHE NEVER DREAMED THAT A CAREER IN QUILTMAKING WOULD BE THE RESULT. HER FIRST FEW QUILTS WERE MADE FROM TRADITIONAL PATTERNS. AS BARBARA EXPANDED HER QUILTING HORIZONS, SHE DISCOVERED THE EXCITEMENT AND CHALLENGE OF CREATING ORIGINAL DESIGNS.

BARBARA LIVES IN JACKSON, WISCONSIN, WITH HER HUSBAND, BARRY. THEIR SON, DAVID, LIVES ON HIS OWN NOW, WHICH MEANS THERE IS MORE TIME THAN EVER FOR HIS MOTHER'S QUILTMAKING ACTIVITIES.

BARBARA HAS MANY QUILTING FRIENDS. SHE IS A LONGTIME MEMBER OF WISCONSIN QUILTERS, INC., AND A CHARTER MEMBER OF COMMON THREADS QUILT GUILD.

SHE ALSO TOOK PART IN THE 1993 SILVER DOLLAR CITY CHALLENGE AND THE 1993 AND 1995 CELEBRITY AUCTIONS BENEFITING THE NEW ENGLAND QUILT MUSEUM.

BARBARA IS KNOWN FOR HER AVID INTEREST IN THE HISTORY OF QUILTS AND HER DIMENSIONAL QUILT DESIGNS. SHE ESTABLISHED NORTH WOODS QUILT DESIGNS WITH THE PUBLICATION OF HER FIRST PATTERN IN 1989. SHE FOLLOWED IN THE FOOTSTEPS OF BOTH HER MOTHER AND GRANDMOTHER. ALTHOUGH THEY WERE ACCOMPLISHED NEEDLE ARTISTS, NEITHER ONE QUILTED; HOWEVER, THEY WERE BUSINESSWOMEN WHEN IT WASN'T THE NORM TO BE A WOMAN IN THE WORLD OF BUSINESS. THEIR EXAMPLES GAVE BARBARA THE INSPIRATION TO TRY SOMETHING NEW AND DIFFERENT.

Quilt Size: 52" x 58"

Materials: 42"-wide fabric

3/4 yd. light fabric for block backgrounds

2 1/4 yds. medium fabric for alternate block backgrounds

1 1/4 yds. dark for lattice, stars, and binding

1/4 yd. medium dark fabric for inner border

5 plaid fat eighths for coats and hoods

Scraps of skin-tone fabrics for faces

Scrap for beards and moustaches

Scraps of 5 trim fabrics

Scraps of brown and charcoal for boots

Scrap of stripe for pants (#3)

Scrap of brown for pouch (#4)

Scrap of navy blue for collar and gown (#5)

3 1/2 yds. for backing

56" x 62" piece of batting

Continued on page 62.

Materials continued from page 61.

¾ yd. paper-backed fusible web

¾ yd. of stabilizer

25 yds. bearding wool/mohair

12" wool yarn for moustaches

6 wooden stars

1 gold star button

12" heavy cotton yarn or string

1 button

Piece of plush felt for boots (#3 optional)

8 plastic eyes (flat on one side)

3 to 4 sheets 14" x 19" template plastic

Cutting

From the light fabric, cut:
　5 squares, each 12½" x 12½", for blocks
From the medium fabric, cut:
　1 square, 23" x 23"; cut twice diagonally to make
　　4 setting triangles
　2 squares, each 13¾" x 13¾"; cut each square
　　once diagonally to make 4 corner triangles
　48 squares, each 1¼" x 1¼", for stars
　48 rectangles, each 2" x 3½", for stars
　48 squares, each 2" x 2", for stars
　1 strip, 6½" x 22½"
　2 strips, each 6½" x 28½"
From the dark fabric, cut:
　12 squares, each 3½" x 3½", for stars
　96 squares, each 2" x 2", for stars
　8 strips, each 2½" x 12½", for sashing
　2 strips, each 2½" x 14½", for sashing
　3 strips, each 2½" x 42", for sashing
From the medium dark fabric, cut:
　5 strips, each 1½" x 42", for inner border

Appliquéing the Father Christmas Blocks

1. Trace the silhouette of each Father Christmas onto a 12½" x 12½" light background square, centering the figure on the diagonal. Trace around the figure lightly with a marking pencil.
2. Using a dry iron, fuse a piece of paper-backed fusible web a little larger than each appliqué shape onto the wrong side of the appropriate fabric.

Note: If you use plush, felt, or another napped fabric for boots, do not use fusible web. Glue or sew the boots in place.

3. Make a plastic template for each piece.
4. Reverse each template, trace it onto the paper backing of the fusible web, and then cut out each piece with scissors.

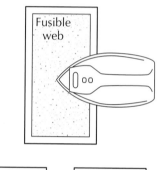

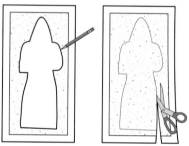

5. Remove the paper from the appliqué pieces for Father Christmas #1 and place them on the background fabric in the appropriate positions. Fuse them to the background in numerical order. Repeat for the rest of the figures.

Note: Before fusing the hand of figure #2, place the 12" length of cotton yarn under it.

6. Cut a piece of stabilizer for each Father Christmas about 2" larger than the figure. Pin the stabilizer to the wrong side of each block; this will prevent the satin stitching from causing puckers.

7. With a marking pencil, mark the arm lines on each figure and the lines where the cuffs overlap on #1 and #5. For accuracy, you can trace the lines onto a paper or plastic template and use a small hole punch to make holes along the lines. Place the template on the figure and make dots in the holes with a marking pencil. Connect the dots to form the correct line. Satin stitch along the lines.

8. Satin stitch the pieces for each block to the background. Vary the width of the satin stitch, using the widest stitch for boots, trousers, and coats, and the narrowest for beards, moustaches, and pouches.

9. Once all the appliqués have been satin stitched, remove the stabilizer.

Assembling the Quilt

1. Sew the 2½" x 42" strips together end to end and cut 2 strips, each 2½" x 44½".

2. Arrange the pieces of the quilt top as shown.

3. Sew the sashing strips, blocks, and setting triangles together in diagonal rows; then sew the rows together. Add the corner triangles last. Once the quilt top is assembled, press, and then square and trim to 44½" x 44½".

Making the Star Blocks

1. Place a 1¼" square of medium background fabric on the corner of a 3½" square of dark fabric, right sides together. Sew across the small square from corner to corner. Trim to a ¼"-wide seam allowance and press open. Repeat with the remaining corners to make the center unit.

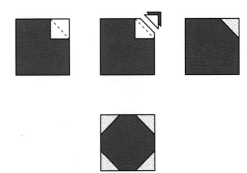

Make 12.

2. Place a 2" square of dark fabric on the end of a 2" x 3½" rectangle of medium background, right sides together. Sew from corner to corner across the dark square. Trim to a ¼"-wide seam allowance and press open. Repeat with another 2" square at the other end of the rectangle to make a Flying Geese unit.

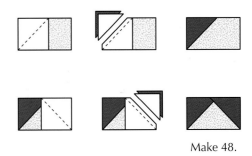

Make 48.

3. Sew Flying Geese units to opposite sides of the center square.

4. Sew 2" squares of medium background to each end of the remaining Flying Geese units; then add 1 unit to each side of the center unit to complete the star.

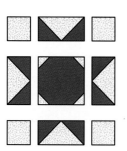 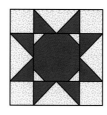

Make 12.

Adding the Borders

1. Sew the 1½" x 42" medium dark strips together as needed to make 2 strips, each 1½" x 44½", and 2 strips, each 1½" x 46½".

2. Sew the shorter strips to the top and bottom of the quilt top and the longer strips to the sides.

3. Sew the Star blocks and the 6½"-wide medium background strips together as shown to make the outer borders. Add them to the top and bottom of the quilt top, and then to the right side.

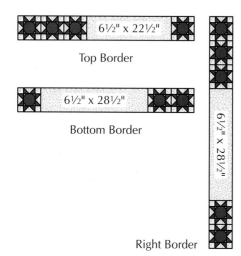

6½" x 22½"

Top Border

6½" x 28½"

Bottom Border

6½" x 28½"

Right Border

Finishing

For detailed finishing instructions, refer to pages 85–87.

1. Layer the quilt top with batting and backing; baste.
2. Quilt as desired.
3. Bind and label your quilt.

Embellishing the Figures

You may think of many other embellishments for each Father Christmas. Here are just a few ideas.

1. For the faces, use dots of craft glue to attach eyes or beads.

2. For the cheeks, apply blush to the face with a cotton swab.

3. For moustaches, cut a piece of wool yarn approximately the length of the moustache. Spread craft glue on the appliquéd moustache. Fluff the yarn and press it into the glue.

4. The beards on figures #2, #3, and #5 are applied in 2 layers. Cover the beard appliqué with glue. Wind yarn around a 1½" x 4" piece of cardboard: the more yarn you wind, the thicker the beard will be. Remove the yarn from the cardboard and press into the glue at the middle of the beard. Repeat and pull the beard up for side burns. When the glue has dried, you can trim and shape the beard with scissors.

5. For eyebrows, place a bead of glue over each eye. Press a small piece of moustache or beard yarn to the glue.

6. For hair, glue a small amount of beard or moustache yarn to figures #2, #3, and #4.

7. For Father Christmas #1, sew a gold star button to his hat trim. For Father Christmas #2, glue 3 wooden stars to the string in his hand. For Father Christmas #4, glue a button to the pouch. For Father Christmas #5, glue stars to the coat.

Crazy Patchwork Angel Pillow

By Lezette Thomason

Crazy Patchwork Angel Pillow by Lezette Thomason, 1995, Nashville, Tennessee, 15" x 15".

LEZETTE THOMASON IS CO-OWNER OF THE CHILDREN'S CORNER, A RETAIL AND WHOLESALE COMPANY THAT SELLS HEIRLOOM SEWING SUPPLIES, WHERE SHE HAS BEEN A TEACHER, DESIGNER, AND WRITER FOR NINETEEN YEARS. SHE TEACHES TWICE YEARLY AT THE MARTHA PULLEN SCHOOL OF SEWING AND IN HUNTSVILLE, ALABAMA. SHE ALSO TEACHES FOR NEEDLECRAFT INTERNATIONAL IN SYDNEY, AUSTRALIA, AT SEWING IN THE BLUE MOUNTAINS. HER FIRST BOOK WITH THAT PATCHWORK PLACE, *VICTORIAN ELEGANCE*, WAS PUBLISHED IN 1996. LEZETTE LIVES IN NASHVILLE, TENNESSEE, WITH HER HUSBAND, MICHAEL, AND THEIR CAT SOCK. SHE HAS A GROWN DAUGHTER, ANNE.

A PILLOW OF OFF-WHITE EMBOSSED SILK IS THE BACKGROUND FOR A HAND-APPLIQUÉD ANGEL WITH A CRAZY-PATCHWORK DRESS. THE DRESS IS MADE FROM WINE-COLORED FABRICS OF DIFFERENT TEXTURES, WITH EMBROIDERY WORKED IN VARIOUS METALLIC THREADS AND RIBBONS. THE PILLOW IS FINISHED WITH A MULTICOLORED FRINGE. AFTER COMPLETING THE PROJECTS FOR *VICTORIAN ELEGANCE*, LEZETTE MADE THIS PILLOW FOR HER HOME.

Pillow Size: 15" x 15"
(not including 1¼"-wide fringe)

Materials: 42" wide fabric

½ yd. fabric for front and back of pillow

½ yd. muslin for backing

¼ yd. lightweight interfacing or muslin for foundation

⅛ yd. gold lamé for angel wings and shoes

Scrap of skin-tone cotton or silk for angel face and hands

Scraps of 5 or 6 assorted fabrics for Crazy patchwork*

¼ yd. of ½- to 1"-wide gold metallic trim for skirt bottom

12" x 12" piece of freezer paper for appliqué

1⅞ yds. of 1¼"-wide fringe

17" x 17" piece of low-loft batting

Narrow metallic gold cording for angel hair

Assorted metallic gold threads, ribbons, and 1/16"-wide specialty cordings for dress and halo**

Gold heart charm

Quilting, chenille, embroidery, and tapestry needles

3 buttons, each ½", for pillow back

16" x 16" pillow form

You need only a small piece of each fabric. Lezette suggests moiré, silk, linen, jacquard, faille, and brocade.

***Size of the thread, ribbon, and cord determines how heavy or delicate your embroidery will look.*

Cutting

From the pillow fabric, cut:

1 square, 17" x 17", for the pillow front

2 pieces, each 12" x 16", for the pillow back.
After the appliqué and quilting is complete,
you will trim these pieces to the correct size.

From the muslin, cut:

1 square, 17" x 17"; use this piece as a backing
when you quilt the pillow front

From the lightweight interfacing or muslin, cut;

1 piece, 8" x 9", for the angel dress

Piecing the Crazy Patchwork

I used foundation piecing to make the Crazy patchwork.

1. Trace the foundation-piecing guide onto tissue
paper. To reverse the pattern, turn over the tissue
paper and trace the lines from the front onto the
back.

2. Place the 8" x 9" piece of interfacing or muslin
over the tissue paper and trace the reversed guide
onto the fabric. (If necessary, use a light table or
window.)

3. From one of the patchwork fabrics, cut a piece at
least ¼" larger on all sides than space #1 on the
guide. Place the fabric on the foundation, right side
up, so that it covers space #1. Pin, making sure the
fabric extends at least ¼" beyond the pattern lines
on all sides.

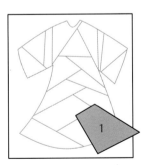

Place piece #1 on
the muslin foundation.

4. From another fabric, cut a piece at least ¼" larger
on all sides than space #2 on the guide. Place this
piece on piece #1, right sides together. Stitch on

the seam line as shown. Trim the seam allowance
to ¼". Fold piece #2 open and press.

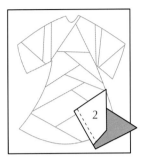
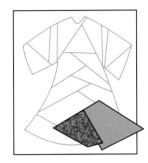

5. From a third fabric, cut a piece at least ¼" larger
on all sides than space #3 on the guide. Place this
piece on pieces #1 and #2, right sides together.
Stitch on the seam line as shown. Trim the seam
allowance to ¼". Fold piece #3 open and press.

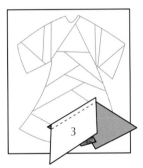
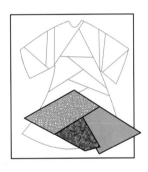

6. Continue stitching the pieces to the foundation
in numerical order until the entire angel dress is
covered. Turn to the back side and staystitch ⅛"
inside the angel outline. Cut out the angel dress.
To keep the edges from fraying, zigzag by machine
around the outside edge.

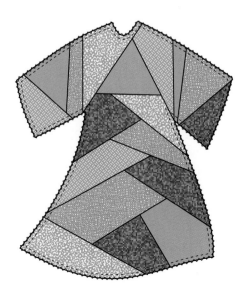

Embroidering the Angel

To reduce bulk and make the angel easier to appliqué, do not embroider into the seam allowances around the angel dress. See pages 99–101 for embroidery stitches.

1. Using a variety of gold metallic threads, ribbons, and cordings, embroider the Crazy-patchwork seams and the flowers and webs. Refer to the pattern for suggestions.
2. Place a terry-cloth towel on your pressing surface. Place the Crazy patchwork right side down on the towel and press.

Appliquéing the Angel

Using the patterns on pages 97–98, make freezer-paper templates of each appliqué piece.

1. The angel dress includes a ¼"-wide seam allowance. Turn the seam allowance to the wrong side and baste in place. Clip where necessary to make smooth edges.
2. Press freezer-paper templates 1–3 to the wrong side of the skin-tone fabric, and then cut out the pieces, adding ¼"-wide seam allowances.
3. Place freezer-paper templates 5, 5 reversed, and 4 on the wrong side of the gold lamé. Using a pressing cloth, press with a *warm* iron to adhere the freezer paper to the lamé. Be very careful! A hot iron can damage lamé. Cut out the shapes, adding ¼"-wide seam allowances.
4. Turn the seam allowances of each appliqué piece to the wrong side of the template and baste in place. It is not necessary to turn under the raw edges that are covered by the angel dress. Handle the lamé gently; it ravels easily.
5. Center the angel dress on the 17" x 17" pillow front. Pin in place. Position the wings, face, hands, and shoes, and then baste in place. When you baste the shoes, remember to allow room for the gold trim at bottom of the dress. Unpin and remove the angel dress. Appliqué the wings, face, hands, and shoes.
6. Baste the angel dress in place, and then appliqué.

Embellishing the Angel

1. Using ¹⁄₁₆" gold cording, outline the bottom edge of each sleeve. Use a tapestry needle to bring the cording up through the fabric and back down.

Couch the cording in place with gold thread. If necessary, tack the cording on the back to keep it in place.

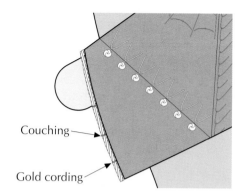

Couching

Gold cording

2. Stitch gold trim to the bottom edge of the dress, turning under the raw edges at each end.

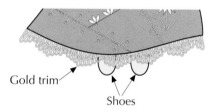

Gold trim

Shoes

3. Using 1 strand of embroidery floss, embroider the face with a back stitch.
4. Stitch the heart charm in place. If you cannot find a charm, embroider a heart with a satin stitch.
5. To embroider the angel's hair, make bullion stitches with fine gold cording. For each bullion stitch, wrap the thread around the needle 18 to 24 times. The trick to making the bullion stitch curve is to make the wrapped thread longer than the stitch. When the stitch is pulled into place, it has to curve, which makes the "hair" strands look soft and natural.

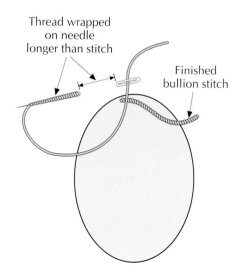

Thread wrapped on needle longer than stitch

Finished bullion stitch

6. For the halo, use ¹/₁₆"-wide gold cording. Using a tapestry needle, pull the cording up at the bottom center of the halo. Couch the cording in place with gold thread, using ¹/₄"-long stitches. Whip the cording around the couched cording between the stitches. Using the tapestry needle, bring the cording to the back of pillow front and tack in place. Using a pressing cloth, press the pillow front.

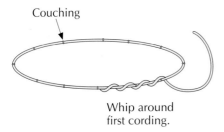

Couching

Whip around
first cording.

Quilting

1. Mark the quilting design on the pillow-front background. Lezette used a 60°-diamond grid with lines 1¹/₄" apart. A 45°-diamond grid or echo quilting would also work well.
2. Layer the muslin backing, batting, and pillow front.
3. Quilt, by hand or by machine, using gold metallic thread.
4. Using a pressing cloth, press the pillow front.

Constructing the Pillow

1. Trim the pillow front to 16" x 16".
2. Stitch the fringe to the right side of the pillow front, aligning the edges and using a ¹/₂"-wide seam allowance.

3. Turn under 1¹/₄" on 1 long edge of a 12" x 16" pillow back; press. Turn under 1¹/₄" again, press, and stitch close to the fold. Repeat with the other 12" x 16" piece.
4. On 1 piece, make a buttonhole in the center of the facing. Make 1 buttonhole 4¹/₄" from each side of the center buttonhole.

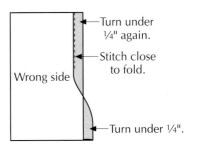

Wrong side

Turn under
¹/₄" again.

Stitch close
to fold.

Turn under ¹/₄".

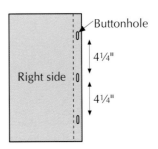

Right side

Buttonhole

4¹/₄"

4¹/₄"

5. Sew corresponding buttons to the other pillow-back piece.
6. Button the pieces together, and then stitch across the overlapped facings, using a ¹/₂"-wide seam allowance. Trim the piece (on all sides) to 16" x 16". Unfasten the buttons.

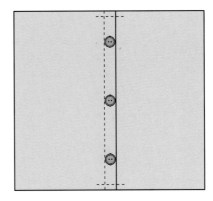

7. Baste the pillow front to the pillow back, right sides together. The fringe will be sandwiched between the pillow front and back. Sew the pieces together, stitching on top of the stitching line for the trim.
8. Turn the pillow cover right side out and press if necessary. Place the pillow form inside the pillow cover and button.

Chickadee Pines

By Deborah J. Moffett-Hall

Chickadee Pines *by Deborah J. Moffett-Hall, 1996, Hatfield, Pennsylvania, 25" x 25".*

DEBORAH J. MOFFETT-HALL

(SEE PAGE 39 FOR AUTHOR BACKGROUND.)

THE INSPIRATION FOR "CHICKADEE PINES" CAME AFTER A VISIT TO DEBORAH'S CHILDHOOD HOME, WHERE HER DAUGHTER, MICHELLE, ADMIRED THE BIRDS VISITING THE NEIGHBORS' FEEDERS. DEBORAH OBSERVED THAT CHICKADEES ARE SOME OF HER FAVORITE BIRDS, AND "POOF," THE DESIGN POPPED INTO HER HEAD.

EVERYTHING FROM THE SKETCH TO THE FABRIC SELECTION CAME TOGETHER SO EASILY THAT THE TOP WAS MACHINE APPLIQUÉD IN ONE EVENING AND MACHINE QUILTED THE NEXT. CREATED ESPECIALLY FOR THIS BOOK, "CHICKADEE PINES" COMBINES A BACKGROUND SQUARE AND THREE BORDERS WITH SIMPLE APPLIQUÉS, SO IT IS EASY TO STITCH ON A MACHINE. THE FINISHED QUILT IS PRETTY ENOUGH TO DISPLAY ALL WINTER LONG.

Quilt Size: 25" x 25"

Materials: 42"-wide fabric

3/8 yd. red print for center square

1/4 yd. red-and-green print
for first border

1/3 yd. red-and-green stripe
for middle border
(or 3/4 yd. of a border print)

1 1/3 yds. medium green print for outer
border, backing, and binding

1/8 yd. or fat quarter each:

Dark green print for leaves

Gold print for pinecones

Brown print for pinecones

Tan print for branch

Assorted scraps of light gray, medium gray,
black, black pindot, and white for bird bodies,
throats, wings, tails, wing tips, and snow

29" x 29" piece of thin batting

Yellow thread or embroidery floss
for bird beaks

Cutting

From the red print, cut:
  1 square, 12" x 12"
From the red-and-green print, cut:
  2 strips, each 3" x 42"; crosscut into 2 strips,
    each 3" x 12", and 2 strips, each 3" x 17"
From the red-and-green stripe, cut*:
  2 strips, each 2¼" x 17"
  2 strips, each 2¼" x 20½"
From the medium green print, cut:
  2 strips, each 2½" x 20½"
  2 strips, each 2½" x 24¼"
  3 strips, each 2½" x 42", for binding
  2 each Leaf 1 and 1 reversed
  2 Leaf 2
  1 Leaf 2 reversed
From the dark green print, cut:
  2 each, Leaf 1 and 1 reversed
  1 each, Leaf 2 and 2 reversed
From the gold print, cut:
  2 Large Pinecones
  2 Small Pinecones
From the brown print, cut:
  1 Large Pinecone
  1 Small Pinecone
From the tan print, cut:
  1 Branch
From the light gray scrap, cut:
  1 Bird Body and 1 Bird Body reversed
From the medium gray scrap, cut:
  1 each Wings 1–3
From the black scrap, cut:
  1 each Markings 1 and 2
  1 each Tails 1 and 2
  1 Wing Tip 1
From the black pin dot scrap, cut:
  1 Wing Tip 2
  1 Wing Tip 3
From the white, cut:
  1 Snow
For mitered borders, cut 4 strips, each 2¼" x 25".

Assembling the Quilt Top

You may want to miter one or all of the three borders. Refer to pages 84–85 for instructions on adding mitered borders.

1. Referring to the quilt diagram for placement, place the snow, and then the branch, on the 12" red square. Appliqué in place.

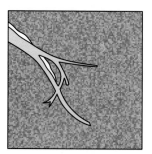

2. Sew the 3" x 12" and 3" x 17" red-and-green print strips to the 12" red square; press the seam allowances toward the outer edges.
3. Repeat with the 2¼"-wide red-and-green stripe strips, and then the 2½"-wide medium green strips.

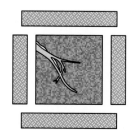 

4. Referring to the quilt diagram, appliqué the remaining pieces to the background in numerical order.
5. Using yellow embroidery floss or thread, embroider the bird beaks by hand or by machine.

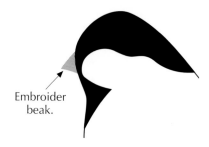

Embroider beak.

Finishing

For detailed finishing instructions, refer to pages 85–87.
1. Press the completed quilt top, and layer it with batting and backing.
2. Baste and quilt as desired.
3. Bind the edges with the remaining 2½"-wide green strips.
4. Label your quilt.

Santa Claus Is Coming to Town—Not!

By Carol Doak

Santa Claus Is Coming to Town—Not! *by Carol Doak, November 1992, Windham, New Hampshire, 40" x 24".*

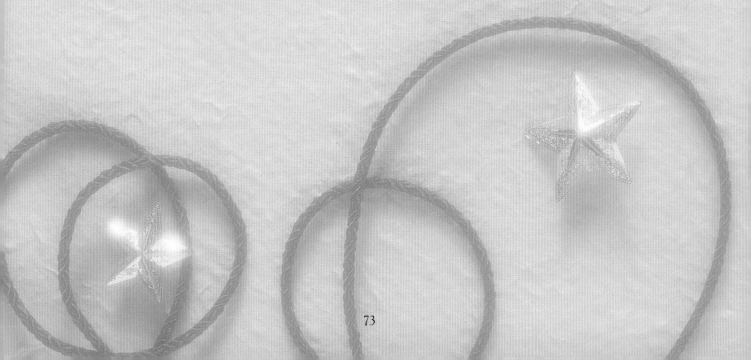

CAROL IS AN AWARD-WINNING QUILTER, POPULAR AUTHOR, AND INTERNATIONAL TEACHER. SHE BEGAN HER QUILTING CAREER IN 1979 BY TAKING AN ADULT EDUCATION CLASS IN WORTHINGTON, OHIO, AND THEN TAUGHT THE SAME CLASS THE FOLLOWING YEAR. SINCE THAT TIME CAROL HAS MADE MORE THAN 150 QUILTS AND CONTINUES TO ENJOY WRITING, TEACHING, AND DESIGNING. SHE CURRENTLY LIVES IN WINDHAM, NEW HAMPSHIRE, WITH HER HUSBAND AND TWO SONS.

CAROL IS THE AUTHOR OF *QUILT-MAKER'S GUIDE: BASICS & BEYOND* (AMERICAN QUILTER'S SOCIETY) AND *COUNTRY MEDALLION SAMPLER*, *EASY MACHINE PAPER PIECING*, *EASY REVERSIBLE VESTS*, *EASY PAPER-PIECED KEEPSAKE QUILTS*, AND *EASY MIX & MATCH MACHINE PAPER PIECING*, ALL PUBLISHED BY THAT PATCHWORK PLACE.

THE INSPIRATION FOR THIS QUILT WAS CAROL'S DESIRE TO DESIGN A HOMESPUN-TYPE QUILT TO HANG OVER THE FIREPLACE DURING THE CHRISTMAS SEASON. SHE DECIDED TO USE THE SONG *SANTA CLAUS IS COMING TO TOWN* AS THE BASIS FOR HER SCENE. SINCE THE HOLIDAY SEASON IS SUCH A BUSY TIME OF YEAR, SHE DESIGNED HER QUILT SO IT COULD BE MADE QUICKLY USING PRIMARILY ROTARY-CUTTING AND MACHINE-PIECING TECHNIQUES.

"WHEN I DREW THE APPLIQUÉ SLEIGH AND PLACED IT IN THE SCENE, THE THOUGHT CROSSED MY MIND THAT, WITH A FEW MINOR ADJUSTMENTS, I COULD PUT A WHOLE NEW TWIST ON THIS FAMILIAR SONG," CAROL SAYS. "THE UNEXPECTED DESIGN GAVE ME A CHUCKLE AS I MADE IT AND PROMPTED MANY CHUCKLES FROM FRIENDS AND FAMILY MEMBERS."

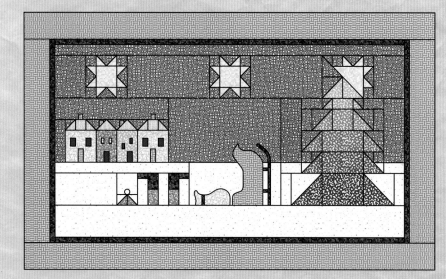

Quilt Size: 40" x 24"

Materials: 42"-wide fabric

½ yd. red check for sleigh, chimneys, 2 doors, and outer border

½ yd. black print for sleigh runners, Santa's boots, bag tie, 2 windows, inner border, and binding

⅓ yd. beige print for snow

½ yd. navy blue print for sky

⅛ yd. blue-and-white print for stars

4" x 12" green print #1 (lightest) for 1 house and tree top

4" x 7" green print #2 for tree

4" x 7" green print #3 for tree

4" x 7" green print #4 for tree

5" x 9" green print #5 (darkest) for tree

⅛ yd. brown print for bag and 2 houses

⅛ yd. red print for Santa's hat, legs, and 1 house

5" x 10" gray print for roofs

Scraps of black solid for 2 doors and 6 windows

Scrap of white-and-black print for 2 windows

Scrap of white solid for Santa's pompon

⅞ yd. for backing

28" x 44" piece of batting

Cutting for Borders and Binding

Fabric	No. to Cut	Dimensions
Red check	2 strips	3" x 19½"
	2 strips	3" x 40½"
Black print	2 strips	1" x 19½"
	2 strips	1" x 34½"
	4 strips	2" x 42"
Beige print	1 strip	3½" x 34½"

Making Row 1

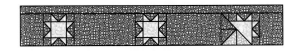

Cutting

Fabric	No. to Cut	Dimensions
Navy-blue print	1 strip	1½" x 34½"
	1 piece	4½" x 8½"
	1 piece	4½" x 7½"
	2 pieces	3½" x 4½"
	11 squares	1½" x 1½"
	1 square	2⅞" x 2⅞"; cut once diagonally to make 2 triangles
	1 square	1⅞" x 1⅞"; cut once diagonally to make 2 triangles*
	3 squares	3¼" x 3¼"; cut each square twice diagonally to make 12 triangles*
Blue-&-white print	2 squares	2½" x 2½"
	10 squares	1⅞" x 1⅞"; cut each square once diagonally to make 20 triangles
	1 square	3⅞" x 3⅞"; cut once diagonally to make 2 triangles*
Green #1	1 square	2⅞" x 2⅞"; cut once diagonally to make 2 triangles

Not all triangles will be used.

Assembly

1. Assemble the whole stars as shown.

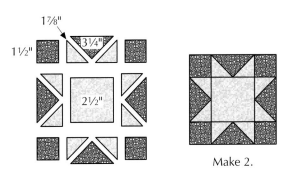

Make 2.

2. Assemble the partial star as shown.

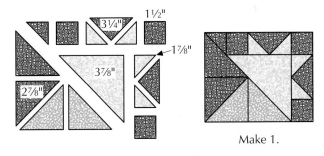

Make 1.

3. Sew the units together to complete Row 1.

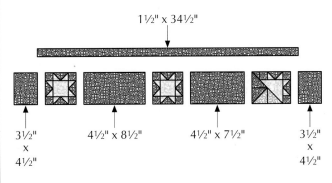

Making Row 2

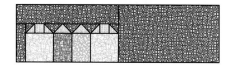

Cutting

Fabric	No. to Cut	Dimensions
Navy-blue print	1 strip	2½" x 11½"
	1 strip	1½" x 4½"
	1 strip	6½" x 11½"
	1 square	3¼" x 3¼"; cut twice diagonally to make 4 triangles*
	1 square	1⅞" x 1⅞"; cut once diagonally to make 2 triangles
Brown print	2 squares	3½" x 3½"
Red print	1 piece	2½" x 3½"
Green print #1	1 piece	2½" x 3½"
Gray print	2 squares	1½" x 1½"
	2 squares	1⅞" x 1⅞"; cut each square once diagonally to make 4 triangles
	1 square	3¼" x 3¼"; cut twice diagonally to make 4 triangles*

Not all triangles will be used.

Assembly

1. Sew the navy blue triangles and the gray triangles and squares together as shown.

2. Sew the red, green #1, and brown pieces together as shown.

3. Join the units with the remaining navy blue pieces to assemble Row 3.

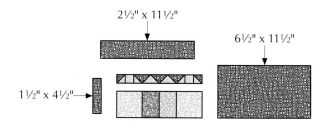

Making Row 3

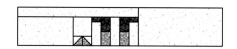

Cutting

Fabric	No. to Cut	Dimensions
Beige print	1 strip	1½" x 13½"
	1 strip	3½" x 6½"
	1 strip	4½" x 9½"
	1 strip	1½" x 3½"
	2 strips	1½" x 3"
	1 square	2½" x 2½"
	1 square	1⅞" x 1⅞"; cut once diagonally to make 2 triangles
Black print	2 pieces	1½" x 2"
	2 pieces	1" x 1½"
Red print	2 pieces	1½" x 2"
	1 square	1⅞" x 1⅞"; cut once diagonally to make 2 triangles

Assembly

1. Assemble the Santa legs and hat.

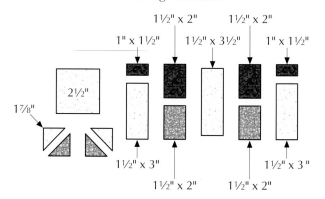

2. Add the beige pieces to make Row 3.

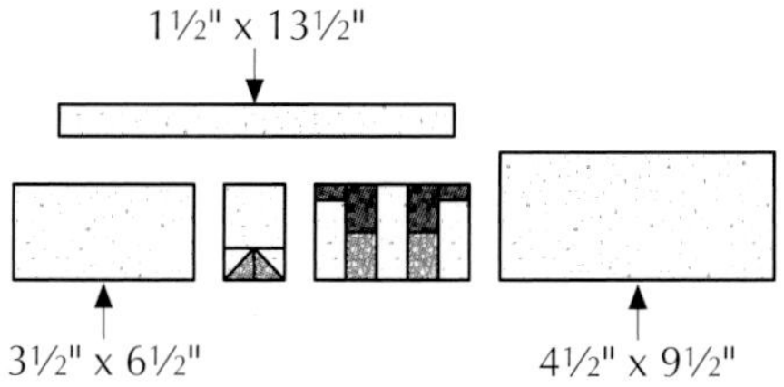
1½" x 13½"
3½" x 6½"
4½" x 9½"

Making the Tree Section

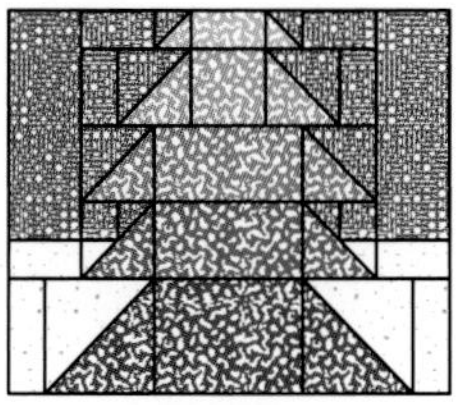

Cutting

Fabric	No. to Cut	Dimensions
Navy-blue print	2 strips	2½" x 6½"
	4 pieces	1½" x 2½"
	2 squares	1½" x 1½"
	2 squares	1⅞" x 1⅞"; cut each square once diagonally to make 4 triangles
	2 squares	2⅞" x 2⅞"; cut each square once diagonally to make 4 triangles
Beige print	2 pieces	1½" x 2½"
	2 strips	1½" x 3½"
	1 square	1⅞" x 1⅞"; cut once diagonally to make 2 triangles
	1 square	3⅞" x 3⅞"; cut once diagonally to make 2 triangles
Green print #1	1 piece	1½" x 2½"
	1 square	1⅞" x 1⅞"; cut once diagonally to make 2 triangles
Green print #2	1 square	2½" x 2½"
	1 square	2⅞" x 2⅞"; cut once diagonally to make 2 triangles
Green print #3	1 piece	2½" x 4½"
	1 square	2⅞" x 2⅞"; cut once diagonally to make 2 triangles
Green print #4	1 piece	2½" x 4½"
	1 square	2⅞" x 2⅞"; cut once diagonally to make 2 triangles
Green print #5	1 piece	3½" x 4½"
	1 square	3⅞" x 3⅞"; cut once diagonally to make 2 triangles

Assembly

1. Assemble the rows of the Christmas tree section as follows:

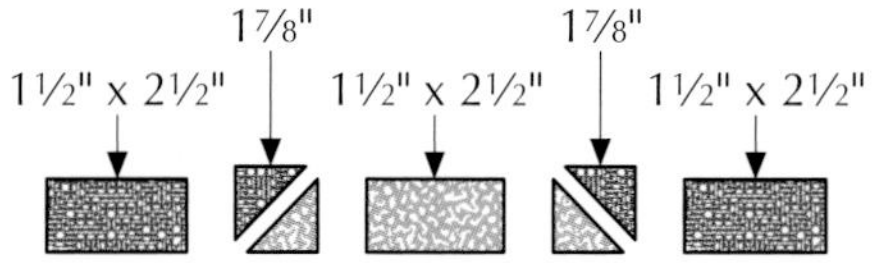
1⅞"
1⅞"
1½" x 2½"
1½" x 2½"
1½" x 2½"

Tree Row 1

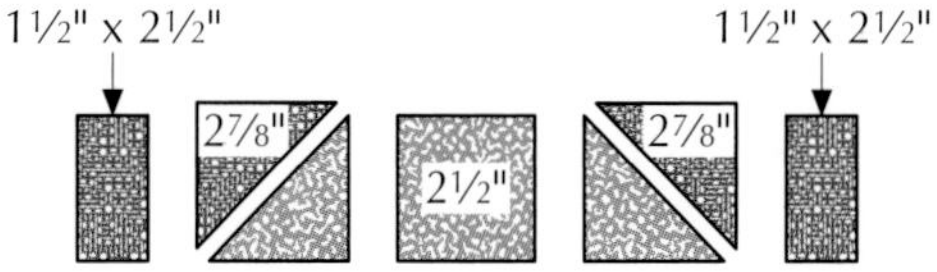
1½" x 2½"
1½" x 2½"
2⅞"
2½"
2⅞"

Tree Row 2

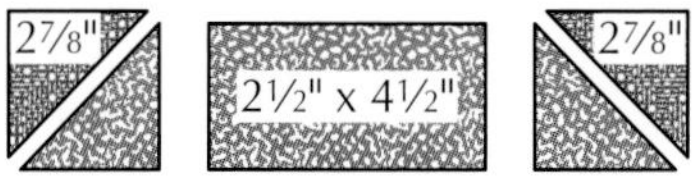
2⅞"
2½" x 4½"
2⅞"

Tree Row 3

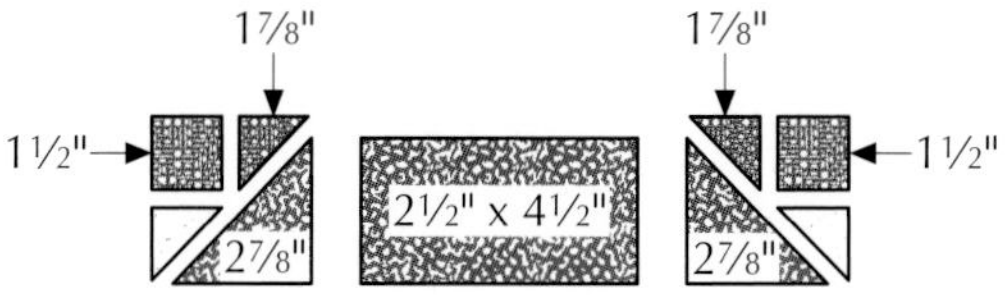
1⅞"
1⅞"
1½"
2½" x 4½"
1½"
2⅞"
2⅞"

Tree Row 4

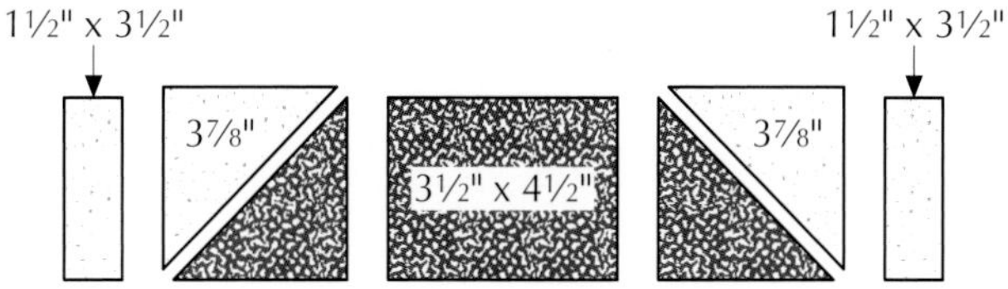
1½" x 3½"
1½" x 3½"
3⅞"
3½" x 4½"
3⅞"

Tree Row 5

2. Sew the rows together and add the side units to form the Christmas Tree section.

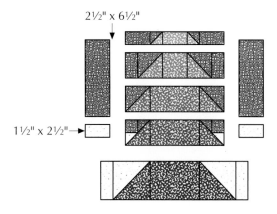

Adding the Appliqués

Door and Windows

In order to catch the bottom edges of the doors in the seam between rows 2 and 3, you need to appliqué the doors before joining the rows. Seam allowances for all appliqué pieces are 1/4" wide.

1. From the black solid, cut a 1½" x 12" straight-grain strip. Fold the strip lengthwise, wrong sides together, and sew along the edge, using a 1/4"-wide seam allowance. Press the seam allowance under the strip.

2. From the black strip, cut 2 pieces, each 1½" long, for the doors on the red and green houses. Pin in place and appliqué, aligning the cut edge of each door piece with the bottom edge of Row 2.

3. From the black strip, cut 4 pieces, each 1¼" long, for the four windows of the brown houses. Pin in place and appliqué.

4. Cut a 1½" x 4" straight-grain strip from the red check. Prepare this strip as you did the black strip. From this strip cut 2 pieces, each 1¾" long, for the doors on the brown houses. Pin in place and appliqué.

5. Cut a 1¼" x 5" straight-grain strip from the red check. Prepare the strip as before. From the strip, cut 4 pieces, each approximately 1" long, for the 4 chimneys. Pin in place and appliqué.

6. Cut one 1" x 3" strip each from the white-and-black and the black solid scraps. Prepare as before. Cut 2 pieces, each 1¼" long, from the black solid for the windows of the green house. Cut 2 pieces,

each 1¼" long, from the white-and-black strip for the windows of the red house. Pin in place and appliqué.

7. Cut a circle, the size of the pompon template on page 104 plus a 1/4"-wide seam allowance, from the white solid scrap. To make the pompon, turn under the seam allowance, baste around the circle, and then pull the thread to gather. Knot the thread. Position the pompon on top of Santa's hat and appliqué.

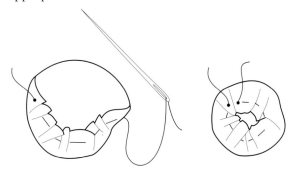

8. Sew Rows 2 and 3 together. Add the Tree section and then Row 1.

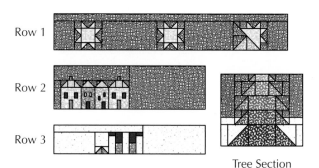

Bag and Sleigh

Using the templates on page 104, cut:
1 Sleigh from the red check
1 Bag from the brown print

Use your favorite method to prepare the pieces for appliqué.

1. Referring to the quilt plan, align the bottom edges of both the sleigh and the bag with the bottom edge of Row 3. Pin the pieces to the background.

2. From the black print, cut 2 bias strips, each 1" x 8". Fold each strip in half lengthwise, wrong sides

together, and sew along the raw edge, pressing the seam allowance flat under the strip.

3. From 1 black bias strip, cut two 1"-long pieces and position them under the sleigh as indicated on the template.

4. Cut a 1½"-long piece and position it at the neck of the bag as indicated on the template. Align the bottom edge of the strip with the edge of the background.

5. Position the remaining strip for the runner, aligning the bottom edge of the strip with the edge of the background. You will catch the strips in the seam when you add the beige strip. Appliqué the pieces, except along the bottom edge.

Finishing

For detailed finishing instructions, refer to pages 85–87.

1. Sew a 1" x 34½" black print strip to the top of the quilt top.

2. Sew a 1" x 34½" black print strip to the 3½" x 34½" beige print strip, and then add them to the bottom of the quilt top.

3. Sew 1" x 19½" black print strips to the 3" x 19½" red check strips. Add 1 to each side of the quilt top.

4. Sew the 3" x 40½" red check strips to the top and bottom of the quilt top.

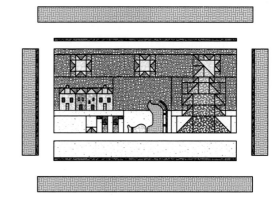

5. Layer the quilt top with batting and backing; baste.

6. Quilt as shown below or as desired.

7. Add a hanging sleeve.

8. Bind the quilt with double-fold binding, using the 2"-wide black print strips.

9. Label your quilt.

Quiltmaking Basics

SUPPLIES

Sewing Machine: To machine piece, you'll need a sewing machine that has a good straight stitch. You'll also need a walking foot or darning foot if you are going to machine quilt.

Rotary-Cutting Tools: You will need a rotary cutter, cutting mat, and clear acrylic rulers in a variety of sizes, including 6" x 24" and 12" x 12". A Bias Square® ruler is helpful for cutting bias squares.

Thread: Use a good-quality, all-purpose cotton or cotton-covered polyester thread.

Needles: For machine piecing, a size 10/70 or 12/80 works well for most cottons.

For hand appliqué, size 10 (fine) to size 12 (very fine) needles work well.

Pins: Long, fine "quilters' pins" with glass or plastic heads are easy to handle. Small 1/2"- to 3/4"-long sequin pins work well for appliqué.

Scissors: Use your best scissors to cut fabric only. Use an older pair of scissors to cut paper, cardboard, and template plastic. Small, 4" scissors with sharp points are handy for clipping thread.

Template Plastic: Use clear or frosted plastic (available at quilt shops) to make durable, accurate templates.

Seam Ripper: Use this tool to remove stitches from incorrectly sewn seams.

Marking Tools: Use a sharp No. 2 pencil or fine-lead mechanical pencil on lighter-colored fabrics, and a silver or yellow marking pencil on darker fabrics. Chalk pencils or chalk-wheel markers also make clear marks on fabric. Be sure to test your marking tool to make sure you can remove the marks easily.

ROTARY CUTTING

Instructions for quick-and-easy rotary cutting are provided wherever possible. All measurements include standard 1/4"-wide seam allowances. For those unfamiliar with rotary cutting, a brief introduction is provided below. For more detailed information, see Donna Thomas's *Shortcuts: A Concise Guide to Rotary Cutting* (That Patchwork Place).

1. Fold the fabric and match selvages, aligning the crosswise and lengthwise grains as much as possible. Place the folded edge closest to you on the cutting mat. Align a square ruler along the folded edge of the fabric. Then place a long, straight ruler to the left of the square ruler, just covering the uneven raw edges of the left side of the fabric.

   Remove the square ruler and cut along the right edge of the long ruler, rolling the rotary cutter away from you. Discard this strip. (Reverse this procedure if you are left-handed.)

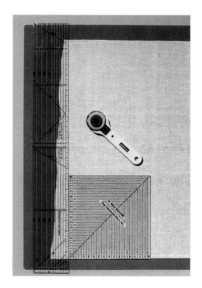

2. To cut strips, align the required measurement on the ruler with the newly cut edge of the fabric. For example, to cut a 3"-wide strip, place the 3" ruler mark on the edge of the fabric.

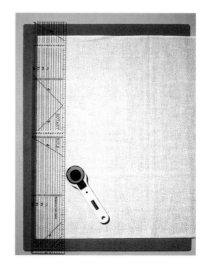

3. To cut squares, cut strips in the required widths. Trim away the selvage ends of the strip. Align the required measurement on the ruler with the left edge of the strip and cut a square. Continue cutting squares until you have the number needed.

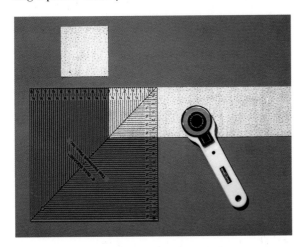

4. Cut squares in half once diagonally for half-square triangles. For quarter-square triangles, cut squares in half twice diagonally.

| Half-Square Triangle | Quarter-Square Triangle |

MACHINE PIECING

Most blocks are designed for easy rotary cutting and quick piecing. Some blocks, however, require the use of templates for particular shapes. Templates for machine piecing include the required ¼"-wide seam allowances. Cut out the template on the outside line so that it includes the seam allowances. Be sure to mark the pattern name and grain-line arrow on the template.

The most important thing to remember about machine piecing is to maintain a consistent ¼"-wide seam allowance. Otherwise, the quilt block will not be the desired finished size. If that happens, the size of everything else in the quilt is affected, including alternate blocks, sashings, and borders. Measurements for all components of each quilt are based on blocks that finish accurately to the desired size plus ¼" on each edge for seam allowances.

Take the time to establish an exact ¼"-wide seam guide on your machine. Some machines have a special quilting foot that measures exactly ¼" from the center needle position to the edge of the foot. If your machine doesn't have such a foot, create a seam guide by placing the edge of a piece of tape, moleskin, or a magnetic seam guide ¼" away from the needle.

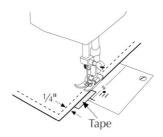

Pressing

The traditional rule in quiltmaking is to press seams to one side, toward the darker color wherever possible. Press the seam flat from the wrong side first, then press the seam in the desired direction from the right side. Press carefully to avoid distorting the shapes.

When joining two seamed units, plan ahead and press the seam allowances in opposite directions as shown. This reduces bulk and makes it easier to match seam lines. Where two seams meet, the seam allowances will butt against each other, making it easier to join units with perfectly matched seam intersections.

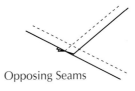

Opposing Seams

APPLIQUÉ

Instructions are provided for three different appliqué methods. Choose one of the following or use your own favorite method.

Making Templates

Templates made from clear plastic are more durable and accurate than those made from cardboard. Since you can see through the plastic, it is easy to trace the templates accurately.

Place template plastic over each pattern piece and trace with a fine-line permanent marker. Do not add seam allowances. Cut out the templates on the drawn lines. You need only one template for each different design. Mark the pattern name and grain-line arrow (if applicable) on the template.

Marking and Cutting Fabric

Place the template right side up on the right side of the appliqué fabric. Leave at least ½" between tracings if several pieces are needed. Cut out each piece, adding a scant ¼"-wide seam allowance around the traced line. This seam allowance will be turned under to create the finished edge of the appliqué. On very small pieces, you may wish to add only ⅛" for easier handling.

The background fabric is usually a rectangle or square. Cut fabric the size and shape required for each project. It is better to cut the background an inch larger than needed in each direction to start, then trim it to the correct size after the appliqué has been sewn in place on the background fabric.

Place the background fabric right side up over the pattern so that the design is centered. Lightly trace the design with a pencil. If your background fabric is dark, use a light box, or try taping the pattern to a window or storm door on a sunny day.

Traditional Appliqué Method

Before sewing appliqués to the background, turn under the seam allowance, rolling the traced line to the back. Baste around each piece. Try looking at the right side of the piece while you turn the edge under, basting right along the fold to catch the seam allowance.

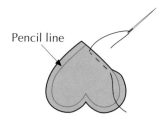

Pencil line

Do not turn under edges that will be covered by other appliqué pieces. They should lie flat under the covering appliqué piece.

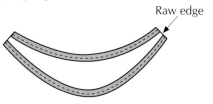

Raw edge

Pin or baste the appliqué pieces to the background fabric. If you have trouble with threads tangling around pins as you sew, try placing the pins on the underside of your work.

Traditional Appliqué Stitch

The traditional appliqué stitch or blind stitch is appropriate for sewing all appliqué shapes, including sharp points and curves.

1. Tie a knot in a single strand of thread that is approximately 18" long.
2. Hide the knot by slipping the needle into the seam allowance from the wrong side of the appliqué piece, bringing it out on the fold line.
3. Work from right to left if you are right-handed, or left to right if you are left-handed.
4. Start the first stitch by moving the needle straight off the appliqué, inserting the needle into the background fabric. Let the needle travel under the background fabric, parallel to the edge of the appliqué; bring it up about ⅛" away, along the pattern line.
5. As you bring the needle up, pierce the edge of the appliqué piece, catching only one or two threads of the folded edge.
6. Move the needle straight off the appliqué into the background fabric. Let your needle travel under the background, bringing it up about ⅛" away, again catching the edge of the appliqué.
7. Give thread a slight tug and continue stitching.

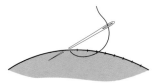

Appliqué Stitch

8. To end your stitching, pull the needle through to the wrong side. Behind the appliqué piece, take 2 small stitches, making knots by taking your needle through the loops. Check the right side to see if the thread "shadows" through the background. If it does, take 1 more small stitch on the back side to direct the tail of the thread under the appliqué fabric.

Stitching Outside Points

As you stitch toward an outside point, start taking smaller stitches within ½" of the point. Trim the seam allowance or push the excess fabric under the point with the tip of your needle. Smaller stitches near the point will keep any frayed edges from escaping.

Place the last stitch on the first side very close to the point. Place the next stitch on the second side of the point. A stitch on each side, close to the point, will accent the outside point.

Stitching Along a Curve

Push the fabric under with the tip of your needle, smoothing it out along the folded edge before sewing.

Stitching Inside Points

Make your stitches smaller as you sew within $1/2$" of the point. Stitch past the point, then return to the point to add one extra stitch to emphasize it. Come up through the appliqué, catching a little more fabric in the inside point (four or five threads instead of one or two). Make a straight stitch outward, going under the point to pull it in a little and emphasize its shape.

If your inside point frays, use a few close stitches to tack the fabric down securely. If your thread matches your appliqué fabric, these stitches will blend in with the edge of the shape.

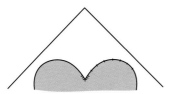

Alternate Appliqué Methods

Needle-Turn Appliqué

This method moves directly from cutting to the appliqué stitch. You do not turn under and baste the seam allowances.

1. Using a plastic template, trace the design onto the right side of the appliqué fabric.
2. Cut out the fabric piece, adding a scant $1/4$"-wide seam allowance all around.
3. Position the appliqué piece on the background fabric; pin or baste in place.
4. Starting on a straight edge, use the tip of the needle to gently turn under the seam allowance, about $1/2$" at a time. Hold the turned seam allowance firmly between the thumb and first finger of your left hand (reverse if left-handed) as you stitch the appliqué to the background. Use a longer needle—a Sharp or milliner's needle—to help you control the seam allowance and turn it under neatly.

Note: Stitches in illustration show placement. They should *not* show in completed work.

Pencil line

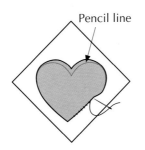

Freezer-Paper Appliqué

Use freezer paper (plastic coated on one side) to help make perfectly shaped appliqués. You can trace around a template or simply trace the design onto the freezer paper. The seam allowances are then turned over the freezer-paper edges and basted or glued to the back side before appliquéing the shape to the background.

1. Place freezer paper, plastic side down, on top of the pattern and trace the design with a sharp pencil.

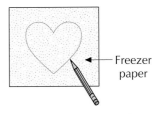

Freezer paper

2. Cut out the freezer paper design on the pencil line. Do not add seam allowances.
3. With the plastic-coated side against the wrong side of the fabric, iron the freezer paper in place, using a hot, dry iron.

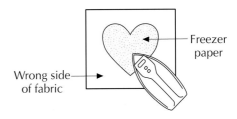

Freezer paper

Wrong side of fabric

4. Cut out the shape, adding $1/4$"-wide seam allowances all around the outside edge of the freezer paper.

5. Turn and baste the seam allowance over the freezer-paper edges by hand, or use a gluestick. (Clip inside points and fold outside points.)

Clip inside corner.

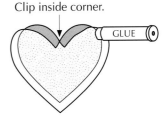

GLUE

6. Pin or baste the design to the background fabric. Appliqué the design.

7. Remove any basting stitches. Cut a small slit in the background fabric behind the appliqué and remove the freezer paper with tweezers. If you used a gluestick, soak the piece in warm water for a few minutes before removing the freezer paper.

BORDERS

For best results, do not cut border strips and sew them directly to the quilt sides without measuring first. The edges of a quilt often measure slightly longer than the distance through the quilt center, due to stretching during construction. Instead, measure the quilt top through the center in both directions to determine how long to cut the border strips. This step ensures that the finished quilt will be as straight and as "square" as possible, without wavy edges.

Plain border strips are commonly cut along the crosswise grain and seamed where extra length is needed. Borders cut from the lengthwise grain of fabric require extra yardage, but seaming the required length is then unnecessary.

You may add borders that have straight-cut corners or mitered corners. Check the quilt pattern you are following.

Straight-Cut Borders

1. Measure the length of the quilt top through the center. Cut border strips to that measurement, piecing as necessary; mark the center of the quilt edges and the border strips. Pin the borders to the sides of the quilt top, matching the center marks and ends and easing as necessary. Sew the border strips in place. Press seams toward the border.

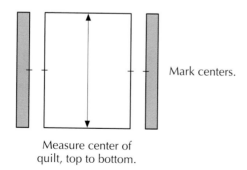

Measure center of quilt, top to bottom.

2. Measure the width of the quilt top through the center, including the side borders just added. Cut

border strips to that measurement, piecing as necessary; mark the center of the quilt edges and the border strips. Pin the borders to the top and bottom edges of the quilt top, matching the center marks and ends and easing as necessary; stitch. Press seams toward the border.

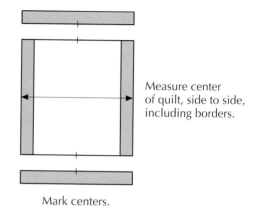

Measure center of quilt, side to side, including borders.

Mark centers.

Mitered-Corner Borders

1. First estimate the finished outside dimensions of your quilt, including borders. Border strips should be cut to this length plus at least $1/2$" for seam allowances; it's safer to add 3" to 4" for some leeway. For example, if your quilt top measures $35^{1}/_{2}$" x $50^{1}/_{2}$" across the center and you want a 5"-wide finished border, your quilt will measure 45" x 60" after the borders are attached.

Note: If your quilt has multiple borders, sew the individual strips together and treat the resulting unit as a single border strip.

2. Fold the quilt in half and mark the center of the quilt edges. Fold each border strip in half and mark the center with a pin.

3. Measure the length and width of the quilt top across the center. Note the measurements.

4. Place a pin at each end of the side border strips to mark the length of the quilt top. Repeat with the top and bottom borders.

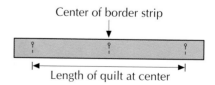

Center of border strip

Length of quilt at center

5. Pin the borders to the quilt top, matching the centers. Line up the pins at each end of the border strip with the edges of the quilt. Stitch, beginning

and ending the stitching ¼" from the raw edges of the quilt top. Repeat with the remaining borders.

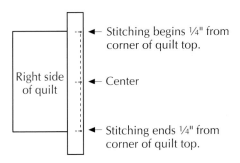

Stitching begins ¼" from corner of quilt top.

Right side of quilt

Center

Stitching ends ¼" from corner of quilt top.

6. Lay the first corner to be mitered on the ironing board. Fold under one border strip at a 45° angle to the other strip. Press and pin.

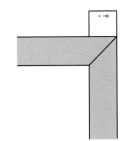

7. Fold the quilt with right sides together, lining up the edges of the border. If necessary, use a ruler to draw a pencil line on the crease to make the line more visible. Stitch on the crease, sewing from the corner to the outside edge.

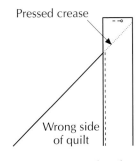

Pressed crease

Wrong side of quilt

8. Press the seam open and trim away excess border strips, leaving a ¼"-wide seam allowance.
9. Repeat with remaining corners.

FINISHING
Marking the Quilting Lines

Whether or not to mark the quilting designs depends upon the type of quilting you will be doing. Marking is not necessary if you plan to quilt in-the-ditch or outline quilt a uniform distance from seam lines. For more complex quilting designs, mark the quilt top before the quilt is layered with batting and backing.

Choose a marking tool that will be visible on your fabric and test it on fabric scraps to be sure the marks can be removed easily. Masking tape can be used to mark straight quilting. Tape only small sections at a time and remove the tape when you stop at the end of the day; otherwise, the sticky residue may be difficult to remove from the fabric.

Layering the Quilt

The quilt "sandwich" consists of backing, batting, and the quilt top. Cut the quilt backing at least 4" larger than the quilt top all the way around. For large quilts, it is usually necessary to sew two or three lengths of fabric together to make a backing of the required size. Trim away the selvages before piecing the lengths together. Press seams open to make quilting easier.

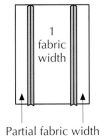

1 fabric width

Two lengths of fabric seamed in the center

Partial fabric width

Batting comes packaged in standard bed sizes, or it can be purchased by the yard. Several weights or thicknesses are available. Thick battings are fine for tied quilts and comforters; a thinner batting is better, however, if you intend to quilt by hand or machine.

To put it all together:
1. Spread the backing, wrong side up, on a flat, clean surface. Anchor it with pins or masking tape. Be careful not to stretch the backing out of shape.
2. Spread the batting over the backing, smoothing out any wrinkles.
3. Place the pressed quilt top on top of the batting. Smooth out any wrinkles and make sure the quilt-top edges are parallel to the edges of the backing.
4. Starting in the center, baste with needle and thread and work diagonally to each corner. Continue basting in a grid of horizontal and vertical lines 6" to 8" apart. Finish by basting around the edges.

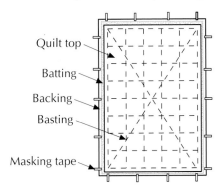

Quilt top

Batting

Backing

Basting

Masking tape

Note: For machine quilting, you may baste the layers with #2 rust-proof safety pins. Place pins about 6" to 8" apart, away from the area you intend to quilt.

Hand Quilting

To quilt by hand, you will need short, sturdy needles (called "Betweens"), quilting thread, and a thimble to fit the middle finger of your sewing hand. Most quilters also use a frame or hoop to support their work. Use the smallest needle you can comfortably handle; the finer the needle, the smaller your stitches will be.

1. Thread your needle with a single strand of quilting thread about 18" long; make a small knot and insert the needle in the top layer about 1" from the place where you want to start stitching. Pull the needle out at the point where quilting will begin and gently pull the thread until the knot pops through the fabric and into the batting.

2. Take small, evenly spaced stitches through all three quilt layers.

3. Rock the needle up and down through all layers, until you have three or four stitches on the needle. Place your other hand underneath the quilt so you can feel the needle point with the tip of your finger when a stitch is taken.

4. To end a line of quilting, make a small knot close to the last stitch; then, backstitch, running the thread a needle's length through the batting. Gently pull the thread until the knot pops into the batting; clip the thread at the quilt's surface.

For more information on hand quilting, refer to *Loving Stitches* by Jeana Kimball (That Patchwork Place).

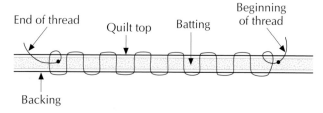

End of thread   Quilt top   Batting   Beginning of thread

Backing

Machine Quilting

Machine quilting is suitable for all types of quilts, from crib to full-size bed quilts. With machine quilting, you can quickly complete quilts that might otherwise languish on the shelves.

Marking is only necessary if you need to follow a grid or a complex pattern. It is not necessary if you plan to quilt in-the-ditch, outline quilt a uniform distance from seam lines, or free-motion quilt in a random pattern over the quilt surface or in selected areas.

1. For straight-line quilting, it is extremely helpful to have a walking foot to help feed the quilt layers through the machine without shifting or puckering. Some machines have a built-in walking foot; other machines require a separate attachment.

Walking Foot

Quilting In-the-Ditch   Outline Quilting

2. For free-motion quilting, you need a darning foot and the ability to drop the feed dogs on your machine. With free-motion quilting, you do not turn the fabric under the needle but instead guide the fabric in the direction of the design. Use free-motion quilting to outline-quilt a fabric motif or to create stippling or other curved designs.

Darning Foot

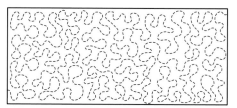

Free-Motion Quilting

Binding

Bindings can be made from straight-grain or bias-grain strips of fabric. For a French double-fold binding, cut strips 2½" wide.

To cut straight-grain binding strips:

Cut 2½"-wide strips across the width of the fabric. You will need enough strips to go around the perimeter of the quilt plus 10" for seams and the corners in a mitered fold.

To attach binding:

1. Sew strips, right sides together, to make one long piece of binding. Press seams open. Join strips at right angles and stitch across the corner as shown. Trim excess fabric and press the seams open.

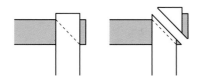

Joining Straight-Cut Strips

2. Trim one end of the strip at a 45°angle. Turn under ¼" and press.
3. Fold the strip in half lengthwise, wrong sides together, and press.

Fold line

4. Trim batting and backing even with the quilt top.
5. Starting on one side of the quilt and using a ³⁄₈"-wide seam allowance, stitch the binding to the quilt, keeping the raw edges even with the quilt-top edge. End the stitching ³⁄₈" from the corner of the quilt and backstitch. Clip the thread.

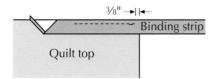

³⁄₈"

Binding strip

Quilt top

6. Turn the quilt so you will be stitching down the next side. Fold the binding up, away from the quilt with raw edges aligned.

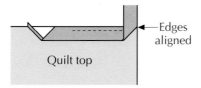

Edges aligned

Quilt top

7. Fold the binding back down onto itself, even with the edge of the quilt top. Begin stitching ³⁄₈" from the edge, backstitching to secure.

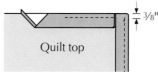

³⁄₈"

Quilt top

8. Repeat on the remaining edges and corners of the quilt. When you reach the beginning of the binding, overlap the beginning stitches by about 1" and cut away any excess binding, trimming the end at a 45° angle. Tuck the end of the binding into the fold and finish the seam.

Quilt top

9. Fold the binding over the raw edges of the quilt to the back, with the folded edge covering the row of machine stitching, and blindstitch in place. A miter will form at each corner. Blindstitch the mitered corners in place.

Quilt back   Quilt back

Signing Your Quilt

Be sure to sign and date your quilt. Future generations will be interested to know more than just who made it and when. Labels can be as elaborate or as simple as you desire. The information can be handwritten, typed, or embroidered. Be sure to include the name of the quilt, your name, your city and state, the date, the name of the recipient if it is a gift, and any other interesting or important information about the quilt.

Templates

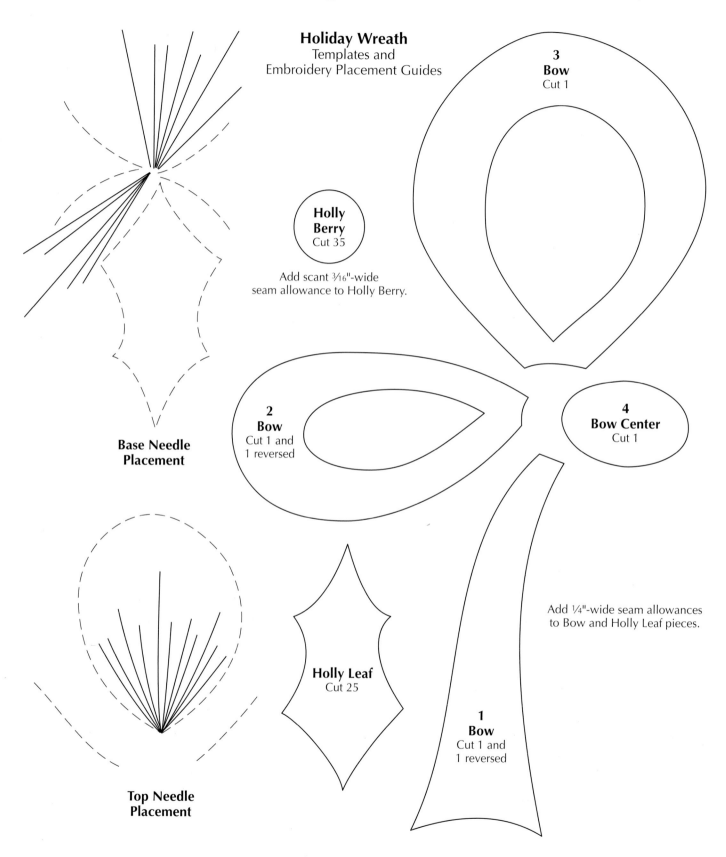

Holiday Wreath
Templates and
Embroidery Placement Guides

3
Bow
Cut 1

**Holly
Berry**
Cut 35

Add scant ³⁄₁₆"-wide
seam allowance to Holly Berry.

**Base Needle
Placement**

2
Bow
Cut 1 and
1 reversed

4
Bow Center
Cut 1

Add ¼"-wide seam allowances
to Bow and Holly Leaf pieces.

Holly Leaf
Cut 25

1
Bow
Cut 1 and
1 reversed

**Top Needle
Placement**

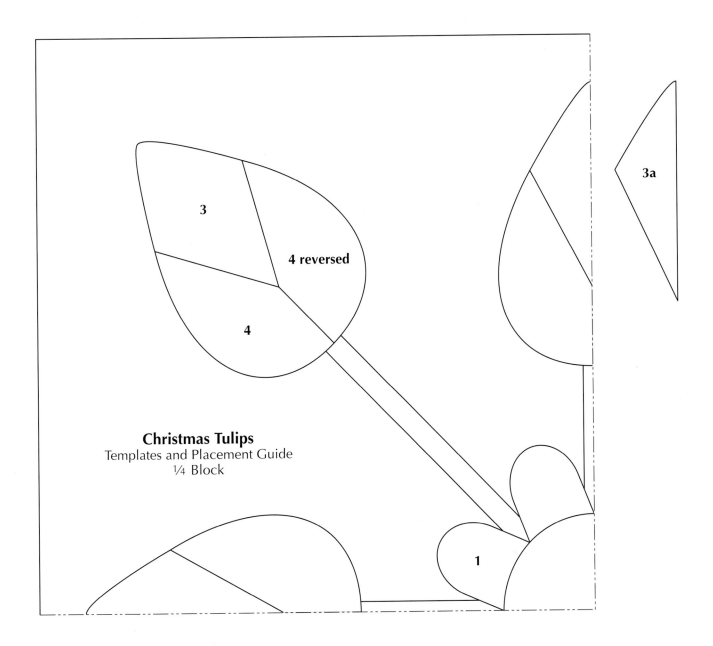

Christmas Tulips
Templates and Placement Guide
¼ Block

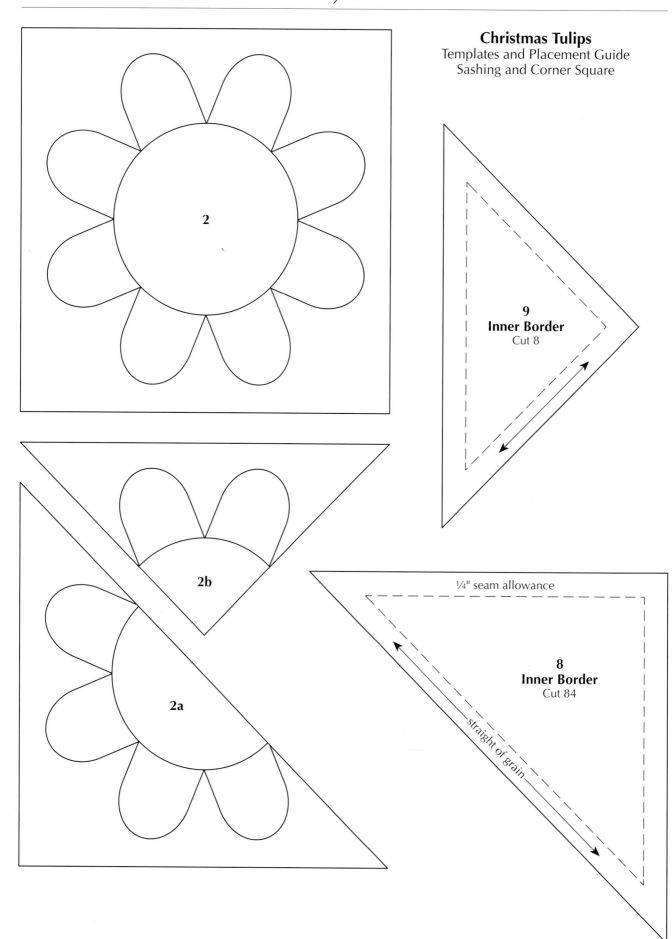

Christmas Tulips
Templates and Placement Guide
Sashing and Corner Square

2

2b

2a

9
Inner Border
Cut 8

¼" seam allowance

8
Inner Border
Cut 84

straight of grain

Holiday Berry Baskets
Templates

Add ¼"-wide seam allowances to all appliqué pieces.

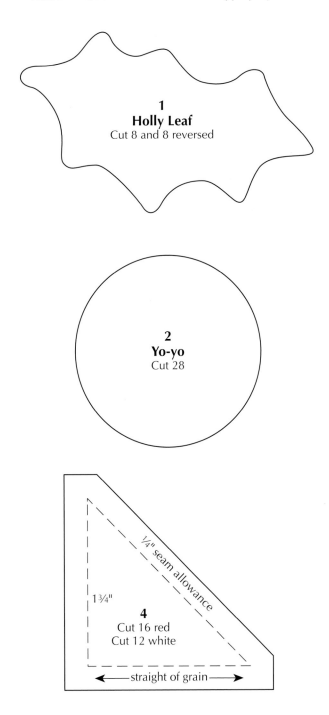

1
Holly Leaf
Cut 8 and 8 reversed

2
Yo-yo
Cut 28

¼" seam allowance

1¾"

4
Cut 16 red
Cut 12 white

←— straight of grain —→

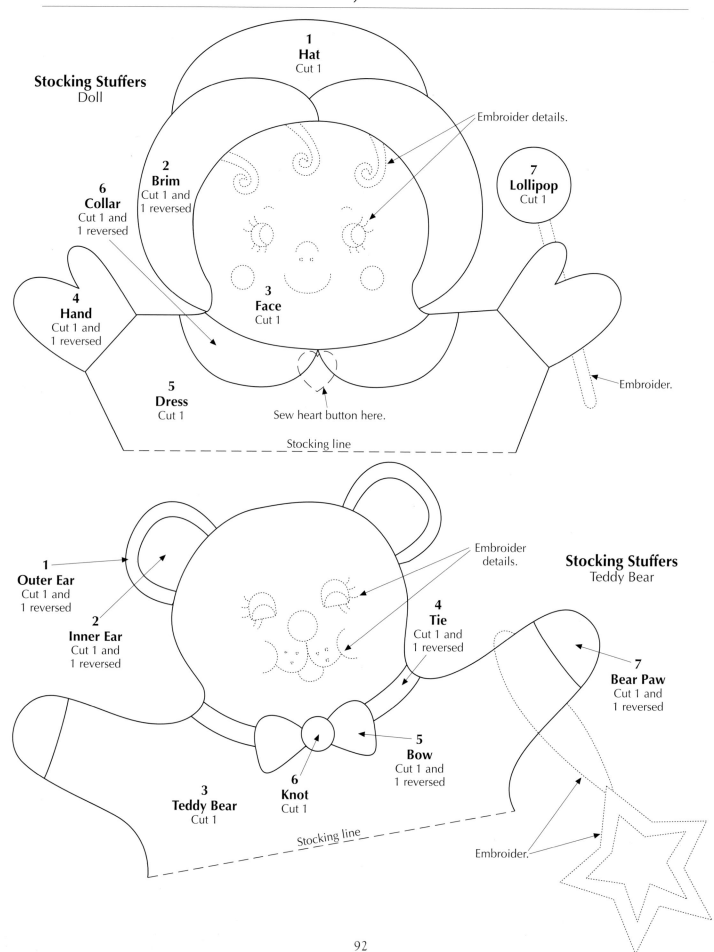

Stocking Stuffers
Doll

1
Hat
Cut 1

Embroider details.

2
Brim
Cut 1 and
1 reversed

6
Collar
Cut 1 and
1 reversed

7
Lollipop
Cut 1

4
Hand
Cut 1 and
1 reversed

3
Face
Cut 1

Embroider.

5
Dress
Cut 1

Sew heart button here.

Stocking line

1
Outer Ear
Cut 1 and
1 reversed

2
Inner Ear
Cut 1 and
1 reversed

Embroider
details.

Stocking Stuffers
Teddy Bear

4
Tie
Cut 1 and
1 reversed

7
Bear Paw
Cut 1 and
1 reversed

5
Bow
Cut 1 and
1 reversed

6
Knot
Cut 1

3
Teddy Bear
Cut 1

Embroider.

Stocking line

92

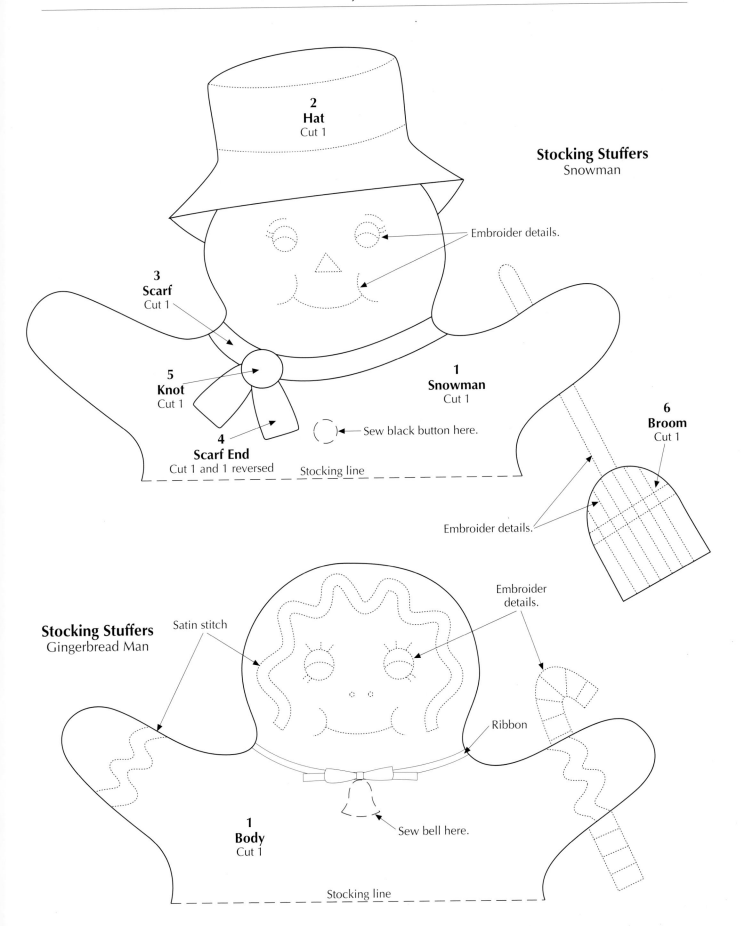

2
Hat
Cut 1

Stocking Stuffers
Snowman

Embroider details.

3
Scarf
Cut 1

5
Knot
Cut 1

4
Scarf End
Cut 1 and 1 reversed

1
Snowman
Cut 1

Sew black button here.

Stocking line

6
Broom
Cut 1

Embroider details.

Stocking Stuffers
Gingerbread Man

Satin stitch

Embroider details.

Ribbon

1
Body
Cut 1

Sew bell here.

Stocking line

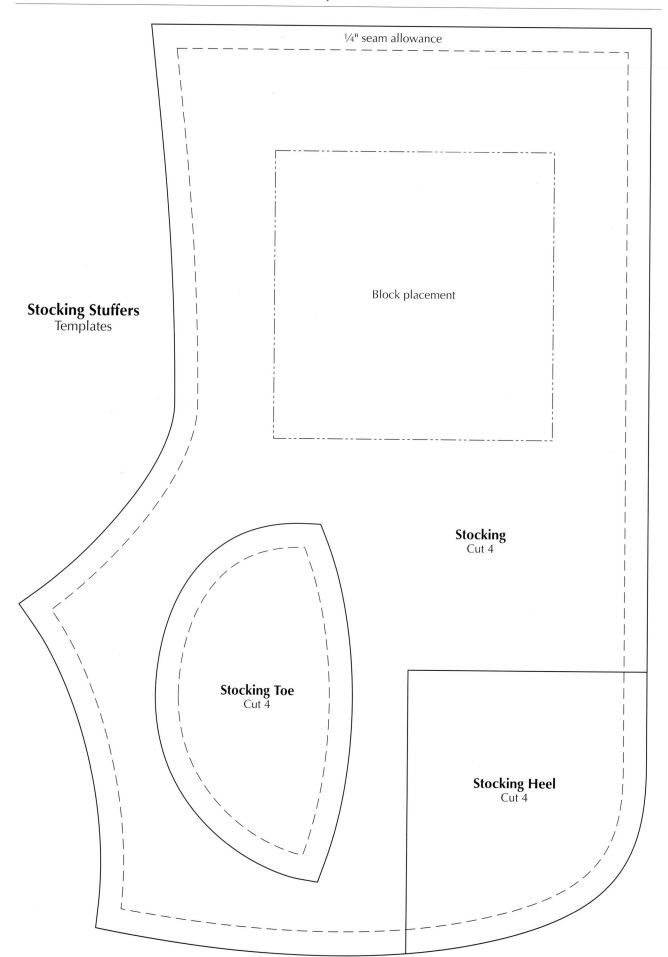

¼" seam allowance

Block placement

Stocking Stuffers
Templates

Stocking
Cut 4

Stocking Toe
Cut 4

Stocking Heel
Cut 4

¼" seam allowance

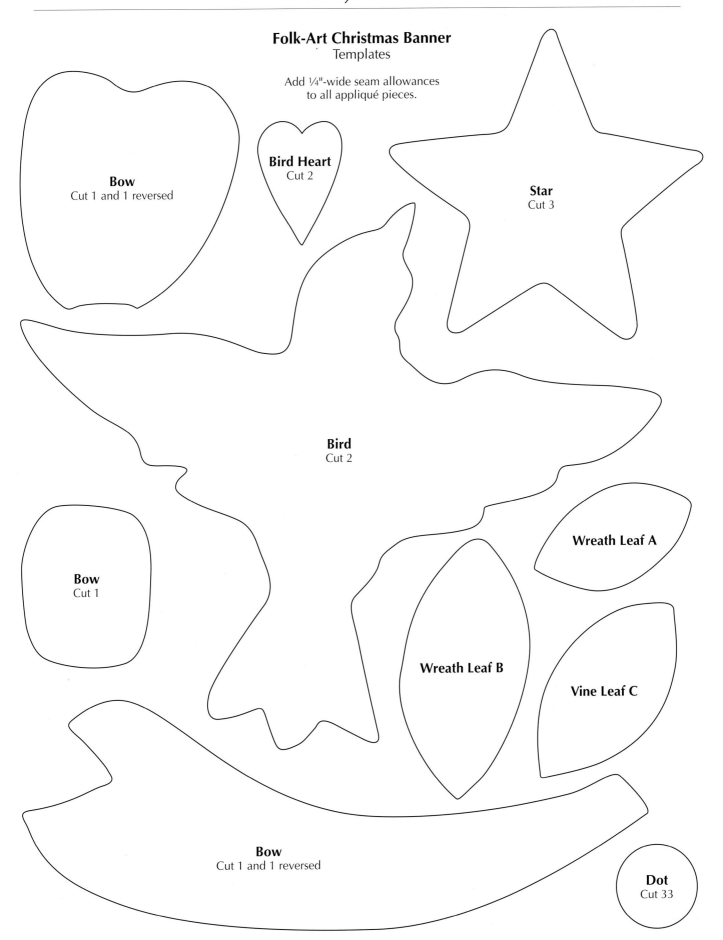

Folk-Art Christmas Banner
Templates

Add ¼"-wide seam allowances
to all appliqué pieces.

Bow
Cut 1 and 1 reversed

Bird Heart
Cut 2

Star
Cut 3

Bird
Cut 2

Bow
Cut 1

Wreath Leaf A

Wreath Leaf B

Vine Leaf C

Bow
Cut 1 and 1 reversed

Dot
Cut 33

Folk-Art Christmas Banner
Templates

Add ¼"-wide seam allowances
to all appliqué pieces.

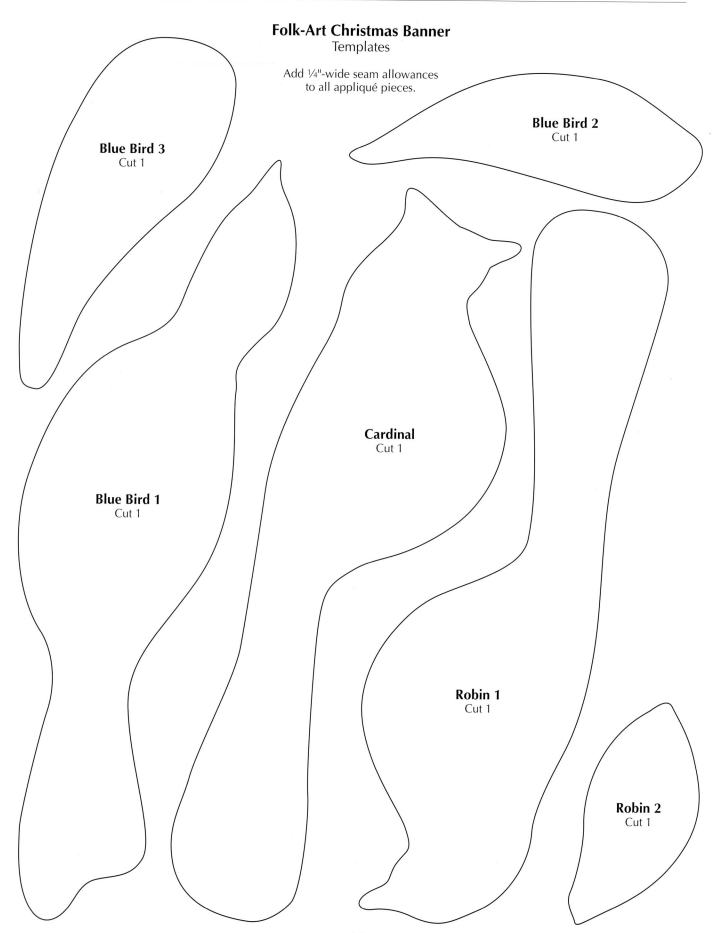

Blue Bird 3
Cut 1

Blue Bird 2
Cut 1

Blue Bird 1
Cut 1

Cardinal
Cut 1

Robin 1
Cut 1

Robin 2
Cut 1

Crazy Patchwork Angel Pillow
Templates and Embroidery Guide

Add ¼"-wide seam allowances to all appliqué pieces.

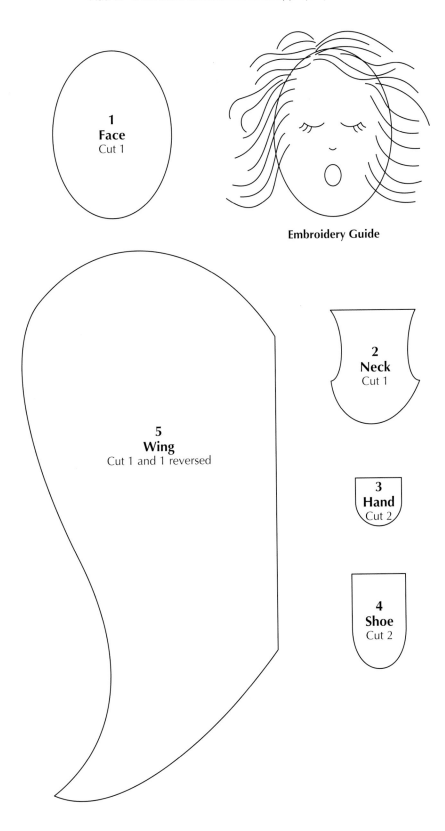

**1
Face**
Cut 1

Embroidery Guide

**5
Wing**
Cut 1 and 1 reversed

**2
Neck**
Cut 1

**3
Hand**
Cut 2

**4
Shoe**
Cut 2

Crazy Patchwork Angel Pillow
Foundation Piecing and Embroidery Guide

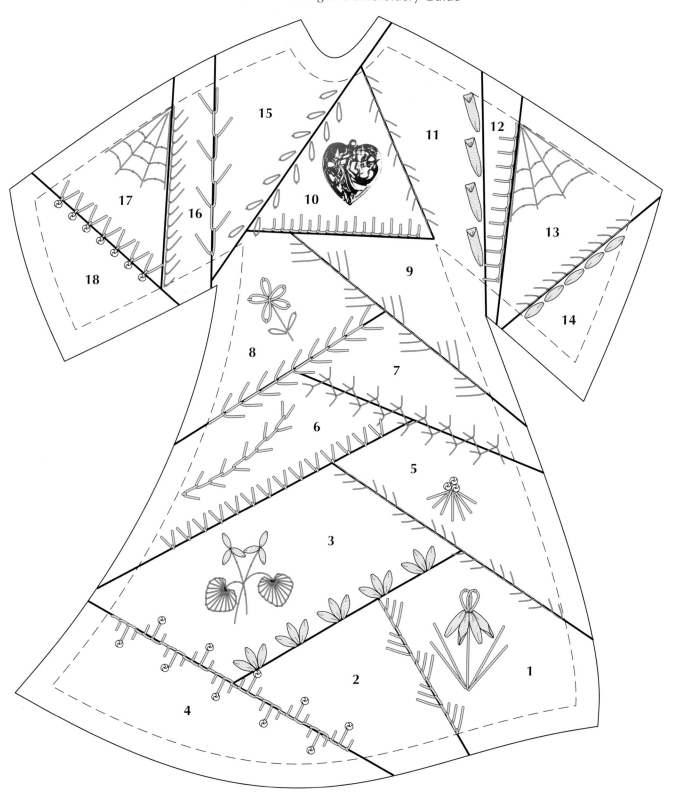

Backstitch

Bullion Stitch

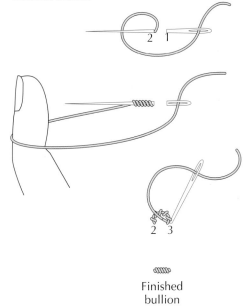

Finished
bullion

Buttonhole Stitch

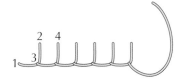

Buttonhole Stitch with Short-Long-Short Stitches, Alternating with Beads of French Knots

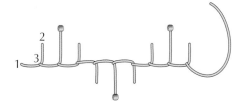

Buttonhole Stitch with Two Stitch Lengths

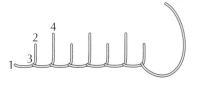

Slanted Buttonhole Stitch

Slanted Buttonhole Stitch, Alternating

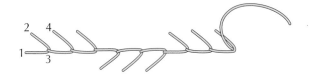

Double Slanted Buttonhole Stitch, Alternating

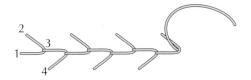

Triple Slanted Buttonhole Stitch, Alternating

Slanted Short and Long Buttonhole Stitch

Single Slanted Buttonhole Stitch with Beads or French Knots

Fern Stitch

Fern Stitch, Alternating

French Knot

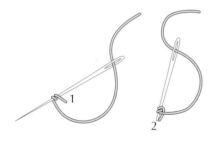

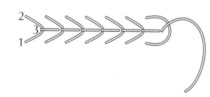

Finished
French knot

Fly Stitch

Grass Stitch
(Three Straight Stitches from One Point)

Lazy Daisy Stitch

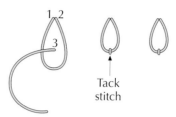

Tack
stitch

Ribbon Stitch

At the end of each stitch, make a loop and pull the ribbon to curl the edges around the point. If you pull the ribbon too tightly, the curls will disappear.

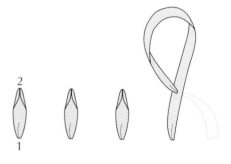

Ribbon Stitch, Looped

At the end of each stitch, make a loose loop. This looks like a curled petal.

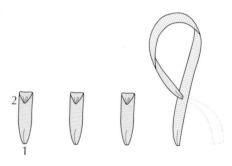

Zigzagged Fly Stitch

Running Stitch with Ribbon

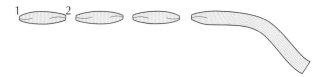

Satin Stitch

Daisy

To make the stem, couch a straight stitch. Use straight stitches or ribbon stitches with silk ribbon to make the petals. Use a cluster of beads or French knots to make the flower center.

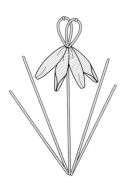

Couching

Iris

Use straight stitches to make the stem and leaves. For the top petals, use lazy daisy stitches. For the bottom petals, use straight stitches and ribbon stitches with silk ribbon.

Spiderweb

To make the web, couch a strand of thread as shown.

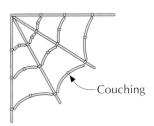

Couching

Violets

To make the stem, couch straight stitches. Use a buttonhole stitch from one point to make the leaves, and straight stitches to make the petals.

Wheat

Using one strand of thread and a slanted buttonhole stitch, work one line of stitches on a curve as shown.

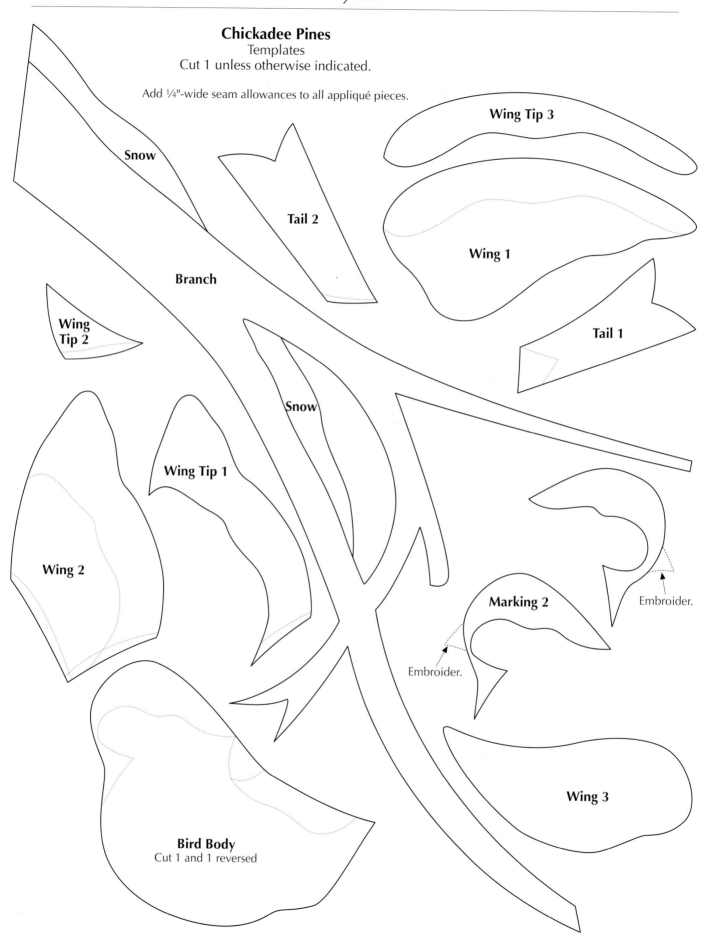

Chickadee Pines
Templates
Cut 1 unless otherwise indicated.

Add ¼"-wide seam allowances to all appliqué pieces.

Snow

Wing Tip 3

Tail 2

Wing 1

Branch

Wing Tip 2

Tail 1

Snow

Wing Tip 1

Embroider.

Wing 2

Marking 2

Embroider.

Wing 3

Bird Body
Cut 1 and 1 reversed

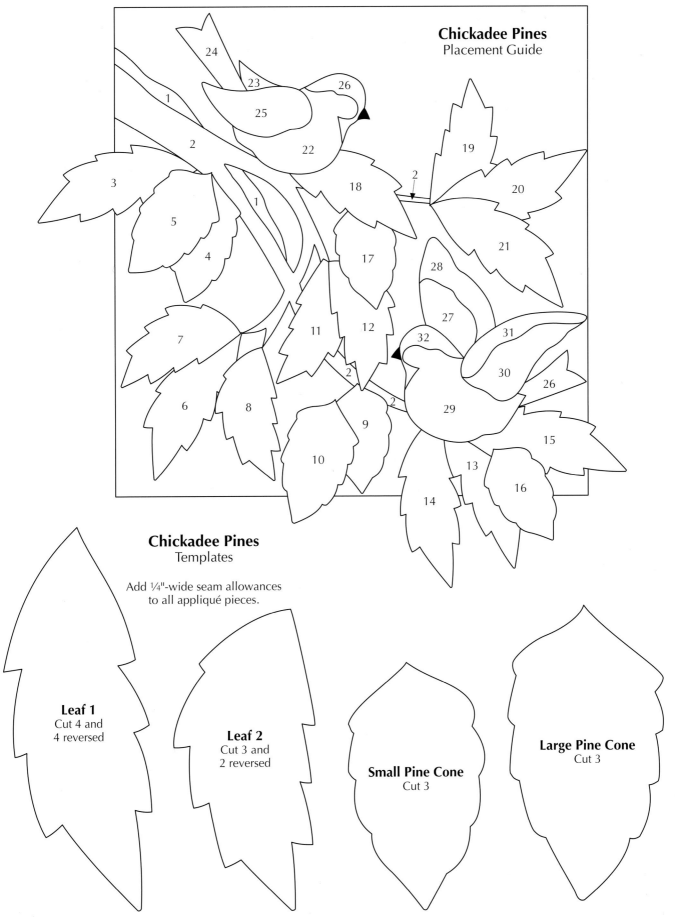

Chickadee Pines
Placement Guide

Chickadee Pines
Templates

Add ¼"-wide seam allowances
to all appliqué pieces.

Leaf 1
Cut 4 and
4 reversed

Leaf 2
Cut 3 and
2 reversed

Small Pine Cone
Cut 3

Large Pine Cone
Cut 3

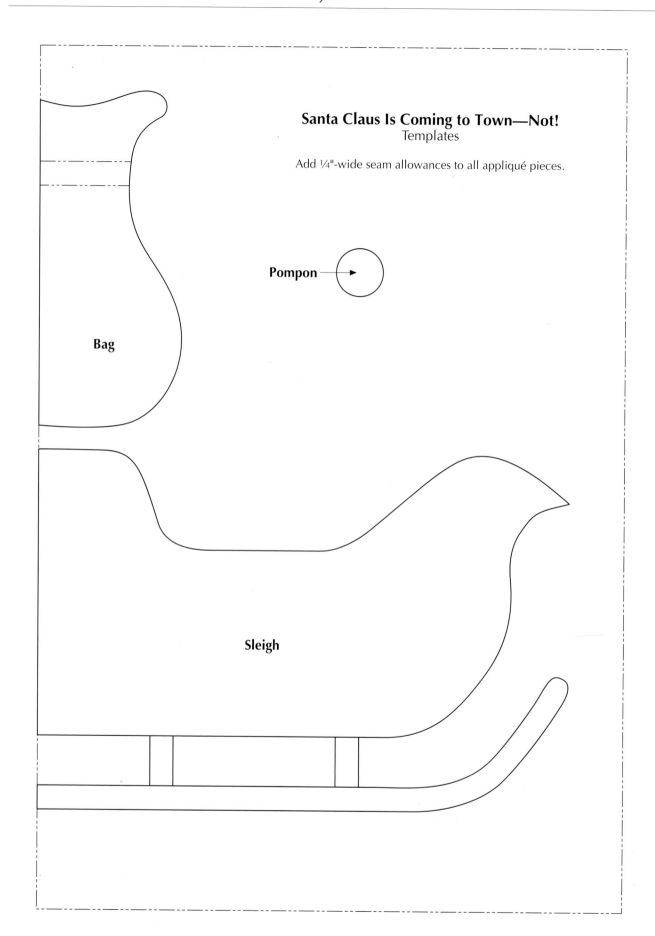

Santa Claus Is Coming to Town—Not!
Templates

Add ¼"-wide seam allowances to all appliqué pieces.

Pompon →

Bag

Sleigh